Edinburgh Review 140

In-Between Places

Edinburgh Review
Editor: Alan Gillis
Assistant editor and production: Jennie Renton
Website and Publicity: Alexandra Sharabianlou
Submissions: Anne Moraa Ondieki and Alexandra Sharabianlou

Advisory Board: Janice Galloway, Kathleen Jamie, Robert Alan Jamieson, James Loxley, Brian McCabe, Randall Stevenson, Alan Warner

Published by Edinburgh Review, 22a Buccleuch Place, Edinburgh EH8 9LN
edinburghreview@ed.ac.uk
www.edinburgh-review.com

Individual subscriptions (3 issues annually) £20 within the UK; £28 abroad. Institutional subscriptions (3 issues annually) £35 within the UK; £43 abroad. Most back issues are available at £7.99 each. You can subscribe online at www.edinburgh-review.com or send a cheque to Edinburgh Review, 22a Buccleuch Place, Edinburgh EH8 9LN

Edinburgh Review 140, *In-Between Places*

ISBN 978-0-9928378-1-5
ISSN 0267-6672

© the contributors 2014
Printed and bound in the UK
by Bell & Bain Ltd, Glasgow

Edinburgh Review
is supported by

ALBA | CHRUTHACHAIL

Contents

Poetry

Fiction

Articles

Reviews

Jackie Kay in conversation with Colette Bryce

CB Jackie, welcome to the special collections department of the Robinson Library at Newcastle University. We're here with the archived material from Bloodaxe Books, the publisher of four of your collections and your selected poems, *Darling*. We have just confronted you with the typescript of your very first collection of poems from 1991, *The Adoption Papers*.

JK [*Opens package*] Amazing. Look at this, it's got its own ribbon! This is quite exciting. Wow, this is like opening up your girl self or something, your past. There's the typescript on top, and the page proofs underneath.

CB Would you say the typescript was done on a word processor or would it have been typed up manually?

JK Typed up manually. I used to type on a Smith Corona, a little electric one that my mum bought me when I was seventeen or eighteen. And then I switched to an Olivetti. It was lovely. You know, with those little spinning...

CB Daisy wheels?

JK Daisy wheel! That's the word I was looking for.

CB Did you get an italics one?

JK Yes [*laughs*] I got an italics daisy wheel. And a ribbon that was half red and half black. It's funny to think of that being really exciting, to have a red ribbon.

CB It was such a tactile experience, dealing with those machines. Everything was just about to change, wasn't it, in terms of the technology around writing?

JK I'm trying to remember when I did get a word processor, it wasn't until a bit later. I had a computer for a while, one of these really old-fashioned ones.

CB And Bloodaxe Books had been around for a few years at that point. What was it about Bloodaxe that made you approach them as a possible home for your first book?

JK Well, I'd got a letter years before from Andrew Motion when he was at – I think it was Chatto. Fred D'Aguiar had told him he should have a look at my poems and he wrote asking to see them. Anyway, he returned them saying he liked things in them but didn't think they were quite strong enough to publish just yet. So that was rejection! [*laughs*] And then they went off to Robin Robertson.

CB Was he at Secker then?

JK Yes, I think he was. He came to a reading I did at the Royal Festival Hall. Do you remember the 'Voice Box'? It was organised by Maura Dooley. Maura gave me my first proper reading there, before I'd ever had a book published. And I remember Robin Robertson coming up to me at that event, saying, 'I've just come to see what this phenomenon is that people are calling Jackie Kay.' [*laughs*] Which made me feel quite nervous! I'd done some readings and they'd gathered their own wind, I suppose. I think of *The Adoption Papers* being first of all performed in different places, and people then wanting to get hold of the book and me saying, 'There isn't a book.' So Robin asked me to send it to him and he promised to get back within three weeks. Which he did, he was true to his word. He said that he liked the book very much and it would probably do well, but nonetheless he didn't feel fully confident in it. And so then I remember ringing him up and asking him, you know, what he meant. And he said, 'Well, it's the difference between grabbing the cock with one hand or grabbing it with two.' Which was an odd thing to say! [*laughs*] He may have been a bit drunk that day because I think James Kelman had just been shortlisted for the Booker. But anyway, I didn't know what that meant.

Kathleen Jamie said to me that it's an old Scottish expression, it's about the bird. But I didn't think that at the time! [*laughs*]

CB [*laughs*] He possibly could have explained that.

JK And I thought it was the strangest form of literary criticism. So then I met Carol Ann and she suggested that I send the poems to Bloodaxe. She bet me a fiver that they would publish them and by this time I was thinking 'Nobody's going to publish them', so I bet her the fiver and she won the bet.

CB It was a good bet…

JK But actually I remember the way that it happened was that Neil wanted to publish quite a large section of 'The Adoption Papers' in an anthology, *New Women Poets*. And I realised that if I published a large chunk of 'The Adoption Papers' in the anthology I would have no chance getting the whole book published. So I said to him that he could only publish that extract if he promised he would publish the whole collection. So I kind of bribed him, really, into publishing that collection.

CB The archived correspondence does show that he was keen, you know, and that the collection developed from there. Originally, was it just 'The Adoption Papers' sequence, and then the idea came to expand the book?

JK Yes, I originally submitted just the sequence, I'd forgotten that. And then Neil said it wasn't quite long enough and did I have any other poems? And I realised that I was already writing what I thought would be my second book, but then I ended up putting the two books together, and I quite liked that it happened that way because it meant that it wasn't just all about adoption. There were different ways in which the themes that came out in the second half of the book mirrored back on to the themes in the first. But the part of the book that gets all of the attention is 'The Adoption Papers' sequence itself.

CB I wanted to ask you about the climate at that time. There are poems in the book about the AIDS crisis, for example, and there's one about donor insemination, lesbian parenting... I remember thinking at the time, as a reader, that this kind of subject matter hadn't appeared in contemporary British poetry before, and in that way the book seemed really suited to Bloodaxe. You seemed to be breaking new ground.

JK Yes, I think Bloodaxe was definitely the right home for *The Adoption Papers*. I think it would have floundered with just about any other publisher because there were things that I was writing about that wouldn't have necessarily been considered 'poetry subjects'. Like donor insemination. Like the AIDs crisis, and Poll Tax...

CB Yes, political engagement as well...

JK Yeah. I think that Bloodaxe allowed you to be a poet with a political ethos and sensibility, and that didn't have to mean that the quality of your poems was threatened. Whereas out in the other poetry world there was this snobbery that if you tackled any issue in a poem it would compromise the poem and make the poem into a polemic. And, you know, political poems do run the danger of turning into polemics, but I tried to find different ways to avoid that in those poems. I think Bloodaxe allowed me to just be myself and to explore and take risks, to make mistakes. The donor poem – I remember thinking, 'I won't include that' because I didn't like it enough as a poem, and then I did include it because I thought it was an interesting poem to be in there with 'The Adoption Papers', to do that mirroring back. I think there are all sorts of ways of exploring what makes us who we are. Identity, nature and nurture are themes I've continued with throughout my whole writing career.

CB You're perceived very much as a Scottish writer, and indeed you use a lot of vernacular Scots in your work. But I've noticed that in your writing life you've always lived at a slight remove from the place. Would you like to say something about that? Do you feel that, in some ways, you're an exile also?

JK I think that's a question I've grappled with most of my life in some way or another. It's fascinating, when you feel a great attachment to the land that you were brought up in, and you feel yourself as part of that land, but that land and that people don't necessarily see you as being part of it. You're constantly aware of that. So you're always being asked where you're from – even now I get asked where I'm from. And even now people don't – in Scotland – *hear* my Scottish accent and they'll say things like 'Are you over from America, dear?' because they see my face. And that becomes quite frustrating. It's funny, and I could tell loads of funny stories about that experience, but ultimately it means that you're questioned at every hurdle. And because you're being questioned all of the time, from being a child right through to a woman in her fifties, it makes you question yourself. It makes you ask that question of yourself, and the question you ask of yourself is in a way more fascinating than the question strangers ask you. So it's not so much the foreigner without that's interesting to me, it's the foreigner within. It's the idea that you feel that the country, in a sense, has both embraced you and not embraced you.

CB It's a very peculiar combination, isn't it?

JK Yes, and it means that you've already got a kind of a Jekyll and Hyde relationship with your own country. On the one hand, yes, you're embraced, and on the other hand you're pushed away. I mean, most writers don't write from a comfortable 'inside' anyway. Most writers find a way to write from the periphery, the margins, the borders, the outside, somewhere or another. Toni Morrison once said 'it's all happening in the borders', that's where it happens. I never think of it as a 'poor me' thing, and I never want it to come across as any kind of self-pity, or even anger, but I do think it's a positioning that is not necessarily voluntary, and not necessarily great socially, but for writing it turns out, paradoxically, to be a good thing.

CB This may be a hard question to answer: where is 'home' for you now?

JK There's an early poem that opens my *Selected* that begins 'My grandmother is like a Scottish pine'. In that poem the grandmother possesses qualities that are wonderful about Scottishness, but she is also racist. And then there's a poem 'Igbo Bath' in my most recent collection where I imagine this Nigerian grandmother that I never met. And in a sense, between these two grandmothers, I belong. I see myself as Scottish, definitely, but also as Nigerian to some extent because my birth father is from Nigeria and I have a developing relationship with the country. I find it fascinating that you can be 'from' a place in inverted commas and not from a place simultaneously, and that your knowledge of a place is completely dependent on other factors. Friendships, family, experience, but also – most importantly of all, really – the imagination. For as long as I remember I had an imaginary Africa in my head that I related to and formed a picture of, and I had an imaginary red dust road leading me in there and out of there. When I got to the eastern part of Nigeria where my birth father was from, his ancestral home, I felt as if my footsteps were on the land already, and all I had to do was walk into these waiting footsteps. And it was quite an epiphany for me, it was a strong, emotional, visceral reaction I had to this red dust road, because it had been the road of my imagination.

CB It had been prefigured in your poems, hadn't it? The red dust road had appeared long before that journey.

JK That's right, and that's the strange thing. Sometimes our imaginary self, our imagination, is up ahead of our real experience or even our real self, our real life. Poetry can walk ahead. I think poetry can lead the way, it can walk ahead even subconsciously even when you're not sure what the hell's going on in your own poem, there can be something that later, with the benefit of hindsight, you can look back on and think 'Oh my goodness, I wrote a poem about that before I actually knew.' For instance, I wrote a poem called 'Pride' where this man on a train, a stranger, looks at my face and says 'Igbo, Igbo definitely.' And that was years before I found out that my father was indeed an Igbo. So I'd written this poem about this imaginary father that was an Igbo, and me being Igbo, and of these people looking at my face and welcoming me as an Igbo, long before I actually found that out.

CB You've spoken before about the influence of African American novelists and poets on you as a young writer and I remember that they – in terms of feminism – were certainly leading the way in those days, authors such as Alice Walker, Toni Morrison, Audre Lorde. Were these writers in some ways your literary mothers and grandmothers?

JK Absolutely, that's a great question. I think that as writers we're little fledgings, aren't we? We don't know that we can fly. But we look up and we look back to people who have actually written work that we really, really admire. And they become perhaps our literary grandmothers, and they teach us how to try and fly, and they teach us that anything can be possible, and to take risks, and to fail and to not be frightened of failure. I remember meeting Audre Lorde who was probably the most influential writer for me – an African American writer, and a lesbian, a mother, somebody who wrote non-fiction and fiction as well as poetry. And I remember reading *The Black Unicorn* in 1981 in Brixton, when Brixton was burning, and just loving the concept of that book, the unity of it, the wholeness of it. And then when I met her a few years after that I was really excited, and at that point in my life I was really identifying myself as black and not interested at all in being Scottish because I felt annoyed that I hadn't really cottoned on properly to being black in any kind of conscious way.

CB In a political way?

JK In a political way, exactly. And then I met Audre Lorde and she said to me, 'You know, you don't have to choose. You can be both. You can be black *and* you can be Scottish.' And that – it seems an obvious thing to say now – but it seemed a very bold thing for me at the time and it was really quite liberating. So, yes, Audre Lorde, Alice Walker, June Jordan, Nikki Giovanni, Lucille Clifton…

CB And not only their writing but how they lived their lives, how they told the truth about themselves, you know? I found them inspiring too.

JK Exactly, and the fact that they all had different relationships with activism and with their own writing. You know, June Jordan, who is dead now, as well as Audre Lorde, also dead, and Alice Walker – they had a fascinating relationship between *doing things* and writing.

CB Going back for a moment to the two grandmother figures, the Scottish one and the Nigerian one, I notice there's a lot of doubling and twos in your work in general, and a theme of twins that runs through. I'm thinking of older poems like 'Pork Pies' and 'Got You', and the duality in the poem 'Somebody Else' from *Off Colour*. In the more recent poem 'Longitude' the speaker takes the hand of a self that might have grown up in Nigeria. Can I ask you about the idea of shadow selves, of doubleness, for you as a person and as a writer?

JK The doppelgänger or other self runs through a lot of Scottish literature so I might have picked up some of that from just being Scottish, that kind of Jekyll and Hyde-ness that goes through *Confessions of a Justified Sinner*. But I think that when you're adopted, you're handed the experience of being double right from the beginning. Right away you have two mothers, two fathers, and two places that you could have been in, perhaps three. Right away you have a relationship with your birth mother that is doubled, you know, you have little facts you know are real facts and then you have an imaginary birth mother you create in your head. So everything is double. You have your family that you're brought up with, and you have this sense of another family, outside of your ken, even, and you don't know if there are brothers or sisters or where they live or anything, but you imagine there might be. So right away when you're adopted you are handed quite a rich imaginative experience, if you want to embrace that. I mean, my brother is also adopted and he didn't want to do that, I know a lot of adopted people who are not interested at all. But I *was* interested, and I was lucky that I had a mum that was fascinated as well with her children's stories. And so, for my mum, what she handed down was a story that she told back to us, and that was in place of genes or mannerisms or genetic traits. It was a story that was handed down and the story was an actual thing. So that story gives you an introduction to doubleness and I think I've always been interested in that. I'm fascinated by twins as well, always have been, and actually that was another strange thing about going to Nigeria, because Igbos are fascinated by twins! That's in the Igbo culture, there's a lot about twins there.

CB Is there a reason for their fascination?

JK Well, they think that twins can be evil [*laughs*]. In the culture it goes right the way back, a kind of superstition. I've always had a fascination with, and a superstitious relationship to, twins and to doubles and to being this other self in the looking glass, the shadow self. The idea that we live our lives in one way, but this shadow self is all the time living its own kind of life. Either imaginatively in a good way, a nurturing way, or in a destructive, negative way.

CB I spoke with another poet about this recently, Julia Copus, and she talked about the concept in quantum physics that when you make a choice another self splits off who made the other choice, and how this becomes an infinite network of possibles.

JK It does, it's a kind of maths, isn't it? Fractions and fractions and bi-fractions...

CB You refer to Frost's 'The Road Not Taken', don't you, in the 'Longitude' poem?

JK That's right. I think we all take that Robert Frost image because it's so resonant to us. It's a metaphor for poetry itself, every single living, writing, breathing poet, and every single dead poet, has made a choice at one point in their lives to take the road less travelled by because that's poetry itself. It kind of haunts me as well, you know? The idea that if I'd been brought up in Nigeria with my Born Again Christian father, whether I would have been like this preachy... preacher, kind of like, nutter? Or if I'd been brought up with my Mormon mother who lives in Milton Keynes, what would I have been like?

CB For a fiction writer, which of course you are as well, it's an amazing tapestry of experience. I'm not surprised that your imagination takes off on these wonderful journeys.

JK And there's a sense that all of our lives are made up of choices made for us and choices that we make ourselves, an odd combination of those two things. Without those choices we might have been different people. If we hadn't fallen in love with this person, or lived in that city, or gone to this university, or done that job, we might have at any point made ourselves into a different person and split off into a whole different *me*! I think that haunts most people, it comes out mostly in our society with love, particularly. People talk about first loves and old loves and romantic loves and if this had gone on, but actually it just spills out into everything. Into culture and racial identity and sexual identity and all the ways that we form ourselves because so much is fate and so much is circumstance. Randomness. And the idea that something so random could make you so thoroughly and completely who you are is fascinating. You know, what if I hadn't been adopted by John and

Helen Kay, but had been adopted by a couple in the army, as my birth mother thought? She was told that I had been adopted by a couple in the army who were taking me abroad, and I think she thought they would be middle class and moneyed and quite posh. Whereas my parents are very working class. The opposite of posh...

CB And communists...

JK And communists, who lived in Glasgow where she lived too for a year. So there she was thinking all the time that she was in Glasgow that I was away.

CB So she also had a fantasy, about you?

JK She did, yes, she thought that I was away in Germany or something. Actually I was just down the road from her. For four years we lived in the same city so that's a strange thing, the proximity of strangeness, you know?

CB You've spoken before about having wanted to be an actress, initially, and now, as a fiction writer, your work is very much concerned with voice and character. Does your flair for character come, perhaps, from that same place, an inner shape-shifter?

JK That's interesting, I think that's right. You know, when you're a writer you get to be some of the things you never got to be, and that's one of the exciting things about it. In your imagination you inhabit the lives of other people and you put yourself in other people's shoes, and even if you don't write dramatic monologues, say if you're a poet, and you don't write in voices, you're putting yourself out into some other experience. But in my case I really love the business of creating a character and their voice. Once I have the voice then I can write the character. If I don't actually have that – the way that they talk – I'm stuck.

CB So it comes from speech, originally?

JK It comes from speech, their speech rhythms and patterns and repetitions, and their idioms.

CB You used Shetland dialect in one poem about a particular speaker. Was it 'The Knitter'?

JK Yeah, that's right, I like experimenting with voice and wherever I go in the world I'm listening to people talk. I've also got one of those memories that can recall whole chunks of conversation more or less verbatim, which makes me not very nice to have an argument with! [*laughs*] Yes, I suppose there's a real voice that you create for your characters, but there's also something else that they have which is, I suppose, a lyric voice or a slightly *unreal* voice, and it's a fusion between these two which then makes up their literary voice. So it's not even so much that you're listening to how a person speaks and putting that down, but trying to find a combination in the way that they speak that gives you something that allows you to soar. That's what I like about creating characters. If I'd been an actress, I'd have learned method acting, or all different kinds of acting, and I find that mysterious because... so many of the actors that I really admire are not necessarily that *articulate* about acting. They hold a lot back from their audience and what can be really powerful are the things that are held back. I've discovered that as a writer. The thing that's really powerful is what your character doesn't say, and what they're unable to say, and to get your reader to, in a sense, try and say it for them. So in *Trumpet,* for instance, you never really find out properly Joss's explanation for living his life as a man when he was born a woman. But you have various ways of looking at that issue from different points of view. So I'd rather get the reader to participate in these characters, almost to have a conversation with the character. And in order for them to do that you need to leave some things unsaid.

CB Thinking about the importance of the monologue in your poetry as well as in your fiction, I'm curious about how you know which form is the right one when a character or 'voice' comes along. Are there dramatic monologue poems that started life as short stories, or vice versa? Do they announce themselves differently?

JK For me, it's always clear whether it's going to be a story or a poem because the idea and the form seem to come together. I know whether it's going to be a poem or a story. I don't know necessarily what form the story will take or the poem will take, I don't know if it's going to be a sonnet for example, but I do know what category it falls into. And even though you could argue about that and say 'Well, "The Adoption Papers" could have been a novel in three parts.' For me, it couldn't have been. You could say that *Red Dust Road* could have been a book of poems. For me, *Red Dust Road* couldn't have been. There isn't any exact science for explaining why you've chosen one form or another, it's more that the form seems to choose you and it comes along with the idea and it's clothed already. It's like the form has walked in, it's already got shoes and a coat and glasses on, or not, and a hat. It's already got stuff on it, the form.

CB You've said that *Red Dust Road* always had to be a prose work, but you also published a collection of poems called *Fiere* alongside it and some of the poems inhabit the same territory as your memoir. Did the importance of that story – travelling to Nigeria to meet your birth father for the first time – require the coming together of all your strategies as a writer?

JK You're absolutely right. When I was writing *Fiere* – I pronounce it *feer* – 'And there's a hand, my trusty fiere, / and gie's a hand o' thine. / And we'll tak a right gude-willie waught / for auld lang syne.' And that's the old Scots word for friend, companion, and it seemed to me when I was writing *Red Dust Road* that the poems were accompanying my journey. I was taking notes for the memoir in prose, kind of diary-type notes, but also there were times when certain things happened that couldn't find a home in prose. So I started writing poems at the same time. I wrote both books at the same time though they got published at different times.

CB So it's about companionship, obviously, the collection of poems, but it's also very much a companion itself to the prose work *Red Dust Road?*

JK Exactly, and if I was to try and explain the difference between the two and why to me something is a poem and why something is a chapter in the memoir, well… In the memoir itself, when I found my birth father, suddenly it felt like my life was a story that was happening *to* me. I didn't need to make it *into* a story, I didn't need to fictionalise it. It already had all of the qualities that stories have!

CB [*laughs*] I've heard you read the episode about meeting him, which can be very funny as well.

JK It already had the drama! It had the mystery, it had the upset, the anger, the passion, all the things that go into making stories. The character, the bizarreness, the strangeness. So there wasn't any real point in making something up. I actually felt compelled to write that book just because of that event, of finding my birth father, and that was the thing that started the whole book off. It took me quite a while to write, to find a tone for writing it that wasn't too bitter or angry.

CB How much time passed between making the journey and publishing the book?

JK Well, there were two journeys. There was the journey where I met my father, and then there was a second one where I met my brother, and they were years apart: 2002 and 2010. I think I started writing the book in 2001 and it was published in 2010. But I wrote a kind of chronological version first and I decided that to ditch that. So I put it in a drawer and I didn't look at it and I started writing the book again episodically, because I realised that the chronology didn't do justice to the complexity of the themes. It tried to pretend that there was a *then* and a *then* and a *then*, and it was more like how our memory goes back and forth. One minute you're seven years old and the next minute you're forty-seven. And there are these epiphanies, or ways in which experiences at seven and at forty-seven, say, can strike exactly the same note. And I wanted to put those kind of things together rather than keeping them apart. So I rewrote the whole book and didn't look at the first one. I was almost too horrified by its badness [*laughs*]. And frightened by it too, you know.

CB Is it still in the drawer?

JK I think I've got it, yeah, because it's fascinating to look at. And then eventually when I finished *Red Dust Road*, the published version, I got out the old one to see if there was anything that I had missed. And there were only a couple of things that I then decided to include in the new one.

CB It's so interesting that you had to have that part of the process, writing a first version, to know what it needed to be.

JK I think writing is frightening in so any different ways. We get frightened of all sorts of things when we write so it's actually quite liberating to write a version of something that will never see light of day, and then to go on and write a completely different version of it. To almost write in secret.

CB With no anxiety about the audience...

JK And no anxiety even about the previous version. Just to write that version and to put it away and to start again maybe with exactly the same theme, the same idea, exactly the same vantage point, but not necessarily looking at it. I think that can sometimes help if you're feeling under pressure and also if you're feeling that you're being forced into looking at something in a certain way. It just opens up the way that you might look at things.

CB I've experienced that in poetry, when you write something with completely the wrong strategy and then, years later, you come back to the same thing but write it utterly differently.

JK Yes, I think all writers will know that feeling where suddenly you have a kind of light-bulb moment where you think 'A-hah!' But during that time when you're in the forest, it's awful.

CB Returning to the things that poetry can do that prose perhaps cannot... Is it a little bit of magical realism that comes into some of the poems? I'm thinking of 'Egusi Soup' where your father just vanishes in the middle of a meal.

JK Yes, in that poem I'm able to let my father turn into fable or myth or fairytale and just fly off at the end of the poem. If you wrote that in prose it would seem rather fanciful. But in a poem, a poem can earn that, and poems can take off at the end. And the same with a poem called 'Burying my African Father' – you know my father is still very much alive. When my dad saw that title in my poetry book he said 'Oh Christ, he's no gonnae like that!' [*laughs*] But in a poem I can imagine my father dead and it not be bitter or vitriolic or too disconcerting for myself or for the reader. If I wrote that as a piece of prose it would seem to have solidified and been made serious. There's something about the form of a poem that can keep things loose around it where people understand its intent, whereas as soon as you commit something to prose, I mean non-fiction prose, in particular memoir prose, you are doing something very different. It's like trying to understand the weight of things and how appropriate some things are. So I think that's an interesting difference between prose and poetry, and that's why prose sometimes can feel so hefty to write. To try and get the lightness and air into prose – that you find in poetry – can be hard.

CB 'Burying My African Father' is a serious poem as well in the sense of putting something to rest, as a writer. I think there's an allusion to Heaney in there about using the pen, if you like, as the instrument of interring him?

JK That's definitely right, and actually one of the last times I read that poem was with Seamus Heaney, and I said to him that there was a nod to him in the poem, and he told me really liked that poem, which was great for me. I had to rush away and take the news into myself privately! [*laughs*] But there's a sense that… After years of imagining my father, and then being confronted with the reality – going from thinking that my birth father might be, as my mum put it, 'a cross between Nelson Mandela and Paul Robeson', to finding this man who regarded me as his 'past sin' and wanted to keep me secret – these two extremes were quite shocking. So that poem in a way finds closure, to use that ghastly American word, where in real life there isn't any. There isn't one, so we invent one. I think all writing is about that to some extent. You invent other possible endings.

CB Even before writing a memoir, you were widely perceived as an autobiographical writer – insomuch as people would consider themselves to have a handful of facts about your life that they'd gleaned from your poetry. But of course, as we know, facts are very elusive in poetry. Do you mind that people often read your poems – or anyone's poems – as truth?

JK Yes, I think I do mind it. I mind being boxed in. Some of that box I might have partly built myself, but I do mind people being too literal. For me, 'The Adoption Papers' sequence isn't an autobiographical work in the strict sense, and people often think it's much more autobiographical than it is. When I wrote it I'd never found my birth father or my birth mother, so all of the facts in there about them are either little facts I'd been told or completely made up. In 'The Adoption Papers' my birth father is called Olubayo. In real life he was called Jonathan! [*laughs*] 'Olubayo was the colour of peat'. There's something quite mythical and grand about him in that way, and so I like that I was using adoption as a theme or as a subject, as a kind of springboard to jump into my imagination. The birth mother's voice is completely made up and the adoptive mother is based on my adopted mum's voice, which is very earthy. I liked the idea that there would be one voice that would be kind of wraith-like and ethereal and hard to pin down, which was the birth mother's, and there'd be another voice that was very substantial and it would be the opposite. The substantial voice was the voice with no supposed biology attached to it, no bloodline, and the insubstantial voice was the voice with the bloodline. So that's what I was interested in trying to create when I wrote 'The Adoption Papers' and the daughter's voice sat somewhere between the two, partly real and partly surreal. People always read 'The Adoption Papers' and think that those things exactly happened. Even my mum! There's a poem about her hiding things in the house before the social worker's visit, hiding evidence of socialism. And she'd told me that she hid things before the social worker's visit but she never actually told me what things. I made the things up, but now she actually thinks she hid those exact things! [*laughs*]

CB [*laughs*] Literature and reality tend to blur after so many years, and nobody knows what was true!

JK No, that's right. We all recognise that from families where we all have different versions of the same truth and actually the truth is multiple. The truth isn't a single version, it's always multiple and I'm fascinated by that. I'm interested in the gathering truth from a number of different voices. Not just 'you were right' or 'you were right', but that if you join all of these voices together, somewhere between this voice and that voice and that voice, you form a truth. And somewhere in the spaces between those voices, or even in the silences, you form something that's true. Particularly with poetry. As soon as you see poetry as being completely autobiographical you reduce its potency. Sharon Olds is a really wonderful writer but she's suffered greatly by people pinning her work to autobiography in a way that she doesn't necessarily want. I mean, she obviously chooses to write up close about her family in a certain way, but…

CB Or appears to…

JK Or appears to, but the truth is always more complex. And actually to really appreciate her work you have to do both. You can't just sort of do the one thing.

CB It's interesting that you've drawn a parallel with Sharon Olds because I know she reacted quite strongly against the term 'confessional poet', which is a dreadful term, very censorious. And she chose, well, she invented an alternative, the 'apparently personal'. In your lyric poems, you have written with apparent candour about love, loss, many life events and experiences, and I'm wondering, does the lyric 'I' in these poems add up to one character? Or does each poem create its own set of terms within which the voice works?

JK It's a fascinating question, and I love the idea of the lyric 'I' and kind of gathering a lyric persona, you know. There's your self, and then there's your own character, and then there's this other self whose voice *is* lyrical. The shadow self's voice is always lyrical, I think. The shadow self doesn't speak broad Glaswegian [*laughs*]. The shadow self is a slightly different voice. And we're always trying to capture, as poets, undertones… And actually when it comes to it the intriguing voices are often not personal to us at all. Not personal in the sense that they're not your mother, they're not your father, they're not you speaking as a child – the authentic voice can have something anonymous about it. And I think it's interesting that we're masked selves. We can hide behind openness and we can also be bold in creating different voices. And that they gather, I suppose, pace over the years. Your own voice as a poet starts to change quite a lot, quite dramatically, and I think that's interesting.

CB That *is* interesting and I don't think we talk about that very often. We're talking twenty-five years of a career, here, and of course it's going to change, isn't it, the lyric voice?

JK Yeah, definitely. And if I look at other poets whose work I really love I'll notice their voices changing massively over time, and them trying to do different things with the voice itself. Or even coming to the conclusion that, say, Don Paterson has done in his poems, that it's not about voice at all.

CB Trying to escape voice?

JK Trying to escape voice, and seeing voice as a kind of tyranny. Trying to escape the nailing down of the voice into something else.

CB Or becoming a persona that we try to project in some way? It's fascinating stuff.

JK I think all writing is a hunt for form and a hunt for language, a hunt for style, and it makes us ask questions all the time. We don't necessarily find the answers.

CB I suppose the very last question ought to be, what next? What are you working on, Jackie?

JK I'm working on a novel at the moment, whose working title is *Bystander*. And it's really, well, saying what novels are *about* always sounds really... [*laughs*]. You take the risk of sounding very stupid. If I'd tried to précis *Trumpet* it would have sounded silly too. But it's about different people that are unconnected, and an event that they all witness, and whether or not they are active or passive in response to that event. So, I'm really interested in how in our society we're now frightened of being active witnesses, in a way that we wouldn't have been even twenty years ago. And how that's forming a different kind of identity, and the way that so much bullying and pressure goes on anonymously, without faces attached to it.

CB Yes, that's been a major change, hasn't it, in our social world?

JK Yes. And 'Bystander', there's a twin in that as well, because of the origins of the word. So I guess this dual thing, well, it's back to dualities in that.

CB It ties in with what you were saying before about the various perspectives and the truth being somewhere in the middle. This kind of event in your novel, it reminds me of the shape of that.

JK Exactly, it's similar. But I do find writing novels the most difficult of all the forms. I find it soul-destroying. I really have to keep telling myself that I can do it, and a lot of the time I think I really can't. Writing a novel for me is definitely the hardest of the forms. You've got to maintain belief in yourself over a longer period, longer than a poem, longer than a story.

CB The long-distance runner?

JK Yeah, exactly. And I think you need self-doubt as much as you need self-belief, but that's the novel for you, it's a real Jekyll and Hyde form. It's like a long disease, actually, it's like experiencing a long illness! [*laughs*] A writing one! I will enjoy when I've finished it. I didn't enjoy writing *Trumpet* either, or *Red Dust Road* particularly. These long pieces of prose are hard, because you have to remember it all! And you think 'Bloody hell, did I write that?' And you have to have big charts up.

CB Do you have charts pinned up in your office?

JK And arrows, yeah. I had a massive chart for *Red Dust Road* connecting this arrow to that arrow. If in doubt, get out some stationery and some brightly coloured pens, a nice big bit of paper. You'll feel like you've done a morning's work!

CB At least it'll look as though you have.

JK Yeah, that's right. If in doubt, get down to the stationery shop!

CB Jackie Kay, thanks so much for talking to us today in the Newcastle University archives.

JK Thank you.

Sasha Dugdale

Do you remember how we chanced upon a home…

Do you remember how we chanced upon a home
A long way from anywhere, with no way of arriving
Or departing, except by foot, as we had come.

We rested in meadow grass that was yellow and thriving
Breaking its way through the once level stone
Sharing its gains with the ragwort and ivy

The poppies and the briar rose.
Memory makes that devastation in our shape
A place of man that man forgoes

And leaves for memory to unmake
In wild creation that masks the hollow eye
And rotting hay and rusty rake

Nothing will ever die
That lives – though all its form be changed –
So there we stopped a bit and lay

And now the hours and days are rearranged
The bodies lying there are beyond strange
Like angels glaring through one peacock eye.

Scylla

A woman was standing in the dark blue water
She could see her breasts but no lower
She could see the raised hairs on her white arms.

The water was still, but massive like machinery
The tide was high and quaking gently
Where an hour before the beach had lain calm

It was so very quiet there, the deep current's suck
And the air so distant and the season so quick
Nothing had passed yet; every change still to come

Only the slight shifts, the peaks and swells
And the ships of clouds bearing unspoken news
All-seeing, all-hearing but always dumb.

Further out two islands where fishermen land
At low tide, and smoke sullen on the sand:
Vanished. The deep water had swallowed them.

The tears wet her eyes, she could have cried
But didn't, knowing it was just the sea inside
Rising through ducts and drains to claim

What belonged to sea and must return
At last to the deep dissolving ocean
Washed clean of every human gain

And shod in silence, supple of shadow
The clouds and birds dark upon its tipping meadow
Without age, without form, without shame.

What am I, sea? A voice, a shape, a soul?
An eerie-pale fish of flesh that stands on soil?
A feather, light as thought? A name?

The sea snatches at her lazily with children-hands
Like it snatches the tatters of salty lands
And wonders if she is some primitive game

The sea has left itself inside fossils
And sent its sinuous fingers to unpeel castles
It would be no matter to pinch out this flame –

Tonight I thought of you…

Tonight I thought of you.

The rain was coming in from the west
But it was still dry and the spindle berries
Wound pink fruit into the harsh cut hedge.
The animals were silent and still as pictures
And the moon was full and almost undressed –
Only a faint line of mist across the naked belly.

**

I walked on the hill and the darkness fell about me
Like heavy rain, and the leaves moved on the earth
Imitating mice and voles and butterflies.

**

It was blacker and blacker in the wood.
The chalk path led into such darkness
My heart almost failed me, but I kept going.

**

The span of a hand from thumb to furthest finger
Is a fraction of the span of a buzzard's wing
The buzzard's bristled neck is far stronger
Than the downy nape of a child sleeping
Which contains in its hollow a sweet cool
And softness as wild and small
As the green slope running down to a pool.
The eye is a poor organ in a poor head
It sees nothing in the evening but throws dark shapes
Into the shadows, it makes night in a deep wood.

**

Mappa Mundi

I know where the white violets grow

        By some unraveling rolls of roof felt

And the orchids, come May,

        I know which slopes they scatter.

I know the field for peewits

        When it's waterlogged and black

And the best, most heady smell

        Of silage, I know where to breathe in.

I know where spindleberries light

        A fence for bryony and a hedge for sloes

The best tracks on a muddy day

        The smell of wet, the badger lurching across

A glow worm, a buzzard, a lark

        The inland egrit, the horse.

There's a den in the copse

        A dead mole, a man with a wound on his face

I know the walk he takes

        The way he clutches his buttock

Another who takes a hockey mask

        To the woods, and wears white gloves.

I know where there are fridges

        Mattresses, old cars and oil cans

And sour tight berries

        Apples and damsons fall ungathered.

How far the dog walkers

        The mothers and toddlers, Sunday ramblers

Their routes, their returns

        I know them all.

The splitting of hair-like streams

                    Names that become accepted

Names that fade like old shops

                    New fences, new asphalt and verges

New signposts, old paths, sudden hills

                    Disappointing smallnesses, surprising drops

Hidden meadows, green waters

                    Holy places, at least to me.

Is the world not like this?

                    An invented place of moving and belonging

A delicious hatred of the other place

                    A sorry love of this one

Bacterial growth along roads

                    Light caught like a thing unwanted in a tree.

How my friend went to look for her roots

It took several trains, a bus ride
along wide roads through a ploughed desert
past empty bus stops many miles apart
to arrive at dusk in a small town.
First wooden houses, the gardens full of cabbages
then grey blocks, the swinging telegraph wire,
unlit bicycles, the damp earth and its suffocating vapours.

This little town had an ancient centre, but nowhere to eat.
The little hotel was shut for repairs a thousand years
in the completing, and the woman who poked her head from
a window said:

– If you're from here then why don't you stay with your family?

– My family left.

So, asked the woman, why come here then? Which, thought
my friend, was a reasonable question, as the darkness came
hard across the open land and up the street and nowhere to
sleep that night
except an empty room where the builders kept their tools,
on a pallet and under a thin blanket.
She slept hardly at all that night, for fear of falling off the
mattress, she rued her purpose and scratched her skin
and vowed she would leave at dawn if she had to walk.

Dawn arrived the pink sky was vaster than anywhere she'd
known. Geography is a strange thing, this town left beyond
the known world, the comfortable road, on the edge of
nothing, from where her family had been plucked
with a million others, carrying only memories of home

walking, walking out of the town.

Villanelle

When an ordinary man dies
Like that, all of a sudden,
There is no darkening of the skies,

Outside the lawns remain green and sodden
And vegetables pulled for supper lie
There is no sudden darkening of the sky

You can see the path his boots have trodden
The boots that slowly fold and subside
When an ordinary man dies

How ordinary! The cats still need feeding
The unbidden sun must endlessly rise
There is no sudden darkening of the skies

The shed is oven warm and full of flies
The beds grow and want weeding
When an ordinary man dies

It is a thing of great surprise
That no curtain is rent, no sacrifice lies bleeding
There is no sudden darkening of the skies

Only the ordinary parting with other lives –
The barely audible tearing of ties
And no sudden darkening of the skies
When an ordinary man dies.

Nicholas Hogg

Vodka Sunday

We first kissed in the bathroom of a film set. Just after she wiped ketchup from her cheek and put her finger in my mouth.

Rufina was cast as a girl addicted to fast food, hiding bags of KFC and McDonald's around the house. I was playing the angry husband who'd forced her onto a diet. It was a stupid short for some hot shot director, a kid with a camera who had me walk through that apartment door about a dozen times before he was happy with the take.

But I needed the hundred dollars. Apart from being told I'd be kissing a girl, the scene was that I come home, discover fries and fast food wrappers on the floor, and search the apartment till I find my girlfriend hiding in the bathroom.

That was the fiction.

The fact was that I'd flown from London to New York, run out of money, and then run out of friends to borrow it from. I planned to waltz into talent agencies with my accent and waltz right out onto film sets. But a few other actors from England had exactly the same idea. Instead I was taking gigs for student directors, sorting casting calls from porn shoots, and eating dollar pizza slices from a place where tramps paid with handfuls of begged nickels and pennies.

Though I always had enough money for a drink.

Before arriving on set I'd nipped in to a local happy hour and necked a couple of vodka cranberries. It was one of those dives you see in 80s films, the kind with neon Bud signs and a barman with rolled up sleeves wiping down the counter, one eye on his tips and the other on a football game. The cliché pouring my drinks nicknamed the vodka cranberries 'thumbcuts' because he topped up the vodka with a splash of juice no bigger than a drop of blood.

Too many thumbcuts and my glassy eyes would give away my drinking. But the two liveners worked a treat for the second scene where I gleefully kicked in the door as instructed, stamping through the splintered wood to find Rufina crouched in the tub eating a cheeseburger.

I had to yank her out by her long blonde hair, and we'd worked it that Rufina grabbed my wrists and stood herself up.

'Still looks tame,' said the director after the third take, pushing his cap further back onto his head.

Rufina arranged her hair in the mirror and talked to my reflection. 'As long as you grab a big handful you can just pull me out.'

She had high, sharp cheekbones, a slightly crooked mouth that she'd tried to paint symmetrical with cherry lipstick, and blue eyes like cerulean at the edge of space.

I told her it'd hurt.

'But this will look better, no?'

She squatted down with the cheeseburger. I paused while the cameraman set his focus, and stood very still over a ketchup-smeared woman in an empty bath.

'Action!'

I did what she asked, took her full weight by her hair and slung her onto the tiles.

'Cut!'

'Sorry, sorry.'

'It's nothing, really.'

I helped her off the floor while the director watched back the take. He stared at the monitor, pulled his cap forward, and then told us we were 'Awesome.'

'See, it was worth it.' Rufina was straightening her clothes, smiling. 'Anyway, I like having my hair pulled.'

What she meant by that, I wasn't sure. But we shot more scenes of me pushing her around, holding her against the wall and shaking her, before I notice some red on her cheek. I think it's blood, feel guilty and beg for forgiveness, pleading that I was only trying to help kick her addiction.

After she puts her finger in her mouth and says, 'It's ketchup,' she puts it in mine. And then we kiss, sugar and tomatoes. All mixed in with the taste of her and a hint of vodka.

'Cut,' interrupted the director.

Now Rufina had lipstick and ketchup smudged around her mouth. And so did I until she reached out with a tissue and wiped it away.

'How was my ketchup kiss?'

I doubt she needed to ask. Blood was pounding around my body.

'Makes me hungry. But not for a burger. The smell of McDonald's makes me sick.'

We scrunched on sidewalks packed with snow. Brooklyn faces, wrapped in scarves and fur-lined Parkas, squinted at the low sun blazing up the avenue. Wind blew directly off the Arctic and whistled up the sleeves of my thin leather jacket. I was cold, but I had money to spend and someone to drink with. And Rufina marched unconcerned into the polar gale with a sheepskin coat buttoned to her chin. She wore one of those hats you tend to associate with Russians, and her white breath rose like smoke from a fire. I wanted to open up that coat and climb inside it with her.

'In Moscow, this temperature is nothing.'

At the Thai place we stamped snow from our shoes and followed a smiling waitress past fake palm trees to a corner table. Rufina lifted off her hat as if it were a crown, ruffled her hair and sat with the regal posture of a girl in finishing school.

'I was in LA for a while,' she was sipping at a lychee cocktail. 'But I missed the cold and the snow.'

'You moved back to Russia?'

'No, no. I missed here, New York. How direct the people are.'

'You mean rude.'

'Maybe. But Russians are the original Americans. We walked across a sea of ice to get here before Columbus.'

I lied. I said I was in New York because work in London had dried up.

'Stage? TV?'

I talked about the mobile theatre, crowds of kids filing into school halls to watch us dumb down Shakespeare. 'I signed autographs on textbooks, hands and juice cartons.'

'You're a big star in their little world.'

I quickly added that I'd memorized four different parts in four different plays, and Rufina raised a carefully plucked eyebrow that I hoped was in admiration, rather than doubt.

And it was probably the vodka and the cocktail, Dutch courage, not bravery, when I gave her the speech of a prince, the skull of a jester. Right there in the restaurant, *Alas, poor Yorick! I knew him Horatio, a fellow of infinite jest, of most excellent fancy.* And no ham actor killing the verse with blustery power. I even wished that bastard from the Guardian had been sitting at the next table with his notebook and pen.

Rufina clapped, lightly, before going back to her drink.

So, no. I didn't tell her about the stage fright. How I'd forgotten my lines before a particularly intimidating Lady Macbeth and struck mute in the middle of a play. Or how the goggle-eyed kids gave in to fits of giggles. Then guffaws. Pantomime laughter from a riot of five year olds. And I certainly didn't tell her that I'd been afraid of the theatre ever since.

'I'm in the wrong productions.' She shook her head, annoyed. 'I should do more acting. That's the thing with TV bullshit, ads and modelling. Nobody asks for an autograph.' She finished her cocktail. 'Just blowjobs.'

'Here,' I said, pushing forward a napkin. 'Sign this.'

She ordered two more drinks before smudging her name with an eye-liner pencil. 'You can sell it on eBay.'

When the food came we'd already finished the second round of cocktails and ordered another pair.

'You made me feel light.'

'When I threw you out the bath?'

'Like a fairground ride,' she shrugged. 'That thrill of flying.'

For a few minutes we just ate, spooning coconut laced with chillies. I hoped the fiery spice might keep my blood from freezing once I stepped back into the cold.

I was kidding myself. She was as tall as me, maybe taller. I wanted to be stood toe to toe with her, naked, in a room where steam hissed from scalding and clanging radiators. Not wrapped in a blanket on the floor of my friend's loft conversion, that Arctic draft reaching under the covers like an icy hand.

'What's the strangest role you've ever played?' She was using the cocktail stick to jab lychees from her glass and pop them between her lips.

'A zombie for a computer game. I was in make up for six hours. I had to sit and watch myself decay in a mirror. They put a hole in my head, flaps of skin falling off my body. Then I died about hundred times in different poses. One kill had my bloody face smeared on a restaurant window.'

'Right now some kid is shooting you.'

'It's a hit game. I'm constantly being murdered in a teenager's bedroom.'

Rufina stopped eating and studied me. 'You're not a zombie.'

I took a chance and dropped the machismo. I was a drunk when I could afford it, and a failed actor when I was half sober. I may as well tell her how scared I'd been to see my mutated reflection and recognize nothing, and that I'd rung up my agent and been told that I'd never work again if I walked off the set.

'I know this feeling better than you think. To see yourself without realising it is you. You understand? Even in your own skin. Last month in Soho, the photographer asks if I want to triple my fee. What was a bikini set is now topless. Next he tells me I can earn five times the agreed price if I take off everything.'

She paused to drink, and I was left wondering how far the shoot had gone.

'And no, I didn't, before you start looking for me on the internet. I liked to scare the jerks by mentioning the Russian mafia, telling them my boyfriend would kill any man who saw me naked.'

I must've looked concerned, because she waved away the idea with her hand.

'Porn offers are normal. My biggest job was for some mascara. I made real money that shoot. For weeks I was waiting to see the ads. But my god, when I did.'

I readied for a tale of model vanity. How a photographer had got the light wrong, the idiot designer who'd dressed her in a size too small.

'I looked great. Fantastic. I saw the posters on the train to Brooklyn. Huge close ups of my eyes. Beautiful.'

'What was the problem?'

'They'd paid for every ad on the carriage. Imagine. In a subway surrounded by your own eyes. Then some of the passengers started looking from the poster to me. I'd been dreaming about this kind of thing for years, you know, a little fame. But it freaked me out. I couldn't breathe. Everywhere I looked I was looking back. I started having nightmares where I'd get on trains and everyone would have my eyes. Old men. Kids. Even dogs. I couldn't catch a train again until I had a friend ride all over town checking I'd been taken down.'

There and then, I told her about my stage fright. Lady Macbeth. All those hanging faces waiting for me to speak. How my beating heart was the loudest sound.

Rufina listened, nodded, and then put down her glass. I'm not sure what I was hoping for. Perhaps a warm hand reaching across the table, polite words of sympathy. Instead she turned and called the waitress, smiling with the icy composure of a Narnian queen.

I spooned up the rest of my curry, staring into the meal as if I might find something written on the bottom of the dish. The instructions for the rest of the evening, lines from a play.

By the time we'd paid the check, great feathers of snow were falling from the blackness. Wads of flakes burst like bags of flour on hitting the sidewalk. Drunk, I could barely see through the blizzard and asked which way Atlantic Avenue was, presuming that was the end of the night.

'I don't care.' Rufina held out her arms and leant back against the wind. 'Let's run with the snow.'

And then she ran. I followed, trying to keep up with her and the swirl of white. We let the gale blow us along, the icy spindrift running out before us like trails of cotton. I felt fantastic, wildly free, as if I were falling headlong with the flakes.

After five blocks we were pluming breath like horses, each gasping exhale whipped away by the breeze.

'Oh, look, look.'

Rufina was pointing at the lady in the harbour, illuminated a gamma ray green on the dark water. On a night like this it was easy to imagine a ship of tired immigrants greeting her as if some seaborne goddess.

'Let's get another drink.'

I was thirsty too. And I wanted to be saved by a statuesque woman. Well, at least inside with her in the warm. Snowflakes blotted my vision, and at this end of Park Slope taco shops sat next to barred liquor stores where alcoholics bought their fix by pointing at labels through bullet-proof glass.

Not that we were so different right then.

Through the white we saw a bar that looked like an Austrian ski lodge, a timber façade with snow fittingly gathered in the windows. Hand in hand we skidded across the road, narrowly missing the charge of a plough scraping and sparking its way along the avenue.

It wasn't an Austrian ski lodge at all. Either I was more pissed than I thought, or had romanticised a log cabin from the whiteout. It was an Irish bar serving hot toddies that steamed like a witch's potion.

'To a day's work,' toasted Rufina. 'Ketchup and kissing.'

We were resting palms on thighs, talking crap because words had nothing to do with what we wanted from the rest of the evening. I hoped. Though we'd kissed on set, and I'd run my hands under her top and over her hips, felt the S-shaped curve at the small of her back, this touch wasn't a command on a script.

'You live in the city?'

I didn't, but I was going wherever she was.

'So, you come with me. Yes?'

We slid into a taxi. The Somali driver sang all the way to the East River, and on the Brooklyn Bridge he wound down his window and let snow flutter around his cab, sticking out his head and laughing at the sky. I saw the deep scars along his cheek, a missing finger and a withered arm, and I laughed at the dark with him. When he veered at the oncoming traffic, and then whipped back the wheel one-handed, Rufina screamed something in Russian before laughing too.

I spent my last twenty paying the fare, which left me without the cash for a train ticket. If Rufina kicked me out I'd be hiking across the bridge through foot-deep drifts.

'Claire, the girl whose apartment this is, wasn't supposed to sub-let.' Rufina put a finger to her lips and pursed a giggly shush as she opened the front door. 'The agency only agreed because Claire said I was her lover and it would be discrimination if they said no.'

We walked to the end of an austere corridor on the third floor, Rufina on tiptoes to stop her boot heels from tap-dancing our arrival to the landlady. Then she clacked open the triple locked entry as if she'd just cracked a safe. What with the snow outside, walking into that room was as good as wandering into Santa's Grotto. Every inch of wall space was filled with pictures, records, clothes, pink feather boas and musical posters.

'Don't tell me she's a showgirl?'

'Guess.' She pointed to a bar hanging from the ceiling by two steel wires.

'A trapeze artist?'

'Well, she calls herself an acrobat.' Rufina stepped forward and clutched the bar with both hands. 'Watch.'

'Careful.'

'Please.'

It was a tiny apartment to have a trapeze dangling from the ceiling. And a tall Russian girl looping her knees over the bar, hanging upside down, and gently swaying back and forth.

'Push me higher.'

I did as I was told, pressing my palms against her sides. She closed her eyes and flopped her arms. Hair swept away from her face, and then over her face. It seemed I'd walked into the workings of a clock, and Rufina was the figurine who performed on the chiming hour.

I asked if she was going to let me have a go.

'You have to earn a ride.'

I had goosebumps at the turn in conversation. 'What do I have to do?'

'Fetch the vodka from the icebox.'

I might well have killed someone if she'd asked. From the kitchen window I could see the shapes of cars beneath their white moulds, a flurry of green flakes turning red above a stop light. New York was empty, the numb streets piled with snow. I never wanted to go outside again. By the time I'd reached into the refrigerator and pulled out the frosted bottle, Rufina was sitting on the trapeze like a spoilt girl on a swing.

'Anything to mix it with?'

'Why ruin the taste?'

I twisted the top and passed her the bottle. She drank it like water.

'I thought vodka and Russians was a stereotype.'

She shook her head and gave me the bottle. 'Like the shy Englishman.'

'I'm not shy,' I protested. 'I'm an actor.'

'Hiding in Hamlet.' She kicked out her feet and swung. 'A computer game.'

I took a sharp, breathless gulp.

'Shy boy.'

She was still swinging. Back and forth, straightening her legs very correctly, then folding them under her body.

'*Shy boy*,' she sang, goading.

'I'm not shy.' I took another, burning mouthful of vodka.

'Really?' She watched me drink again. 'So prove it.'

It was very quiet in the room.

On the stage.

Just the sound of trapeze cables stretching and creaking, the hissing melody of a hot water pipe set deep in the brickwork, pulsing heat and thudding walls, pounding like a heart.

Marianne MacRae

War Biographer

The War paces,
restless in his agitation.
'I'm not all bad, you know?' he says,
turning to me, hands wrung almost to powder.
'I had a life once; parents. Lovers.
But you can't escape destiny, can you?'

He lights a cigarette, sits down to regroup.
Across his face I see the scars so chronicled:
the small, country-shaped burns,
the trenches gouged into his forehead.
His eyes never stop moving.
I find myself drifting across his map.

'Let's talk tactics,' I say.
'Must we? There's so much more to me than that.'
'Okay.' I consider him for a moment.
'Favourite book?'
'The Bridges of Madison County.'
Unexpected. I cross and uncross my legs.
'Movie?' I ask.
'Basic Instinct.'

Are we *flirting* right now?

The War gazes out of the window,
fingers hanging from his hands
like long stems of wheat.
'I'm a very wealthy man,' he says.
'So I've heard.'
'I own a condo in every human heart.
I could take you to yours if you like?'

His eyes are trained on me
and black as bullets.

Human Condition

We do not recall having been
the size of a cashew nut,
though science assures us
we were.

Shelled prawns in dark soup,
no doubt dreaming in escape routes.
Narrow islands of light appearing,
expanding into days.

The burgeoning medals of our eyeballs
flashed with triumph.
We were proud then,
winners.

Hearts bleat wet anthems.
The islands taper,
ready to close
as quickly as they opened.

The Effort Office

Harper tells me he lost his ear in a boxing match, though the scar looks distinctly bomb-shaped. We all have our own secrets and lies I suppose. As he turns, I'm sure I catch a glimmer of brain.

'What's your field experience?' he asks.
'I once caught a rounders ball in my hat.'
'How did that feel?'
'Solid. About as heavy as a small rodent I'd say.'
'Perfect. I think you're going to fit in just fine.'

He stands up and shakes my hand. His skin is smooth and cool and I briefly wonder if he's made of porcelain.

'Your office is on the eighteenth floor. We can take the stairs.'

He hands me one end of a long, thin package with the word **STAIRS** printed on it in Stencil STD, the industrial font. We carry it into the lift and lean it against the mirrored walls. As we ascend the floors, Harper sings a tune about a woman named Judy.

'I have an aunt called Judy,' I tell him.
'Well I have a wife called Judy, and wife trumps aunt so I win.'

We finish the journey in silence.

We come to a door marked 'The Effort Office'. Upon entering the room, I see Maddox crouched in the far left hand corner with his ear pressed to a glass and the glass pressed to the wall.

'That's Maddox,' says Harper. 'There's an empire behind that wall that we're on the verge of conquering. He's doing some reconnaissance work for us.'

Maddox looks at me darkly, with a dark flash of darkest recognition. He twists the glass slightly and looks away.

'This is your desk.'

Harper shows me to a thin plank of wood balanced between two pots of red gloss paint.

'You know what needs to be done. Make up the baskets according to the instructions and send them out by the end of each month. Any questions, just ask Polly.'

He motions towards the mantle-piece, where a hedgehog, fashioned from bits of bark and pinecone and radish, presides over the office. Before I manage to ask whether or not he's insane, Harper has exited the office in a flurry of paper.

Escaping

Here are your instructions:

The hippo will meet you at the corner.
He will blindfold you and lead you towards a town,
a town you have never been to;
one that is built in the cup of an upturned bell.
The hippo will tell you to stay there for a week.
Do not trust the hippo.

Stay there for two days and three nights.
Before dawn on the third day,
find the esoteric man wearing a miniature fez,
and give him the half cigar
hidden in the front of your rucksack.
He will know what to do with it.

You must not speak to this man.
Instead, take tea with his wife;
she will serve crumpets and French fancies
from a two tiered silver platter
and tell you about their son
who is away fighting the war on biographers.

Entertain her intrusive laughter
and if you do so successfully,
she will wrap a grain of rice in a fig leaf
and tell you to travel west.

Go east.

Walk for seven days, but do not rest –

if desperation overcomes you,

eat out the heart of your rag doll;

that should give you all the energy you need.

When the sun sets on the last day,

start digging until you find the tonic.

Drink it.

You will collapse

and fall into a dreamless sleep and then,

nestled in the astrakhan

of a giant Russian lamb,

you will ride until you are home.

On the Author

I like rain more than wind.
I find wind sneaky and treacherous.
Rain is the simpleton of the sky.

I am a wild though consistent liar.

I find most fruit and veg sold in supermarkets to be arrogant.
Loose potatoes still covered in dirt
are the only exception.

When I'm out walking I'm scared I'll snag my hair on a twig
and the whole lot will pull right off my scalp
leaving me bald and dejected.

I have no prejudices:
I hate all people equally.
In winter I build snowmen
so I can punch them in the face.

I have no desire to be a cat,
despite cats being the only cats who know where it's at.

I see birds and reptiles everywhere
and I'm never quite sure what it means,
but who's sure of anything, really?

Yesterday I heard someone
trying to explain how a gate works:

'No, Susan, you just open it and walk through.'
Life is a litany of complex puzzles.

Today I am a caper at a party,
tomorrow I shall be a germ,
the day after that, stomach acid,
and then? Perhaps gastritis.

I tire of myself quickly; every day is like New Year,
I'm always reinventing.

Sometimes I put on a different hat
every day for months on end,
each one a little more wacky than the last.
People like that,
they like it if you're wacky.

Many have questioned my sincerity,
my reality, my depth of feeling.
And I have always answered them,
my voice flat and emotionless,
that I feel.
I really do.

Martin MacInnes

Zoo

Since European intervention in Africa in the fifteenth century primates have been used to assist in the xenophobia at the heart of colonial warfare. Symbolic material expressed in the service of self-identifying nations and species, primates – particularly the four great apes – are presented alternately as anarchic examples of mindless, culture-less flesh, and of dangerously familiar kin.

Global knowledge of apes began with imperialism, as the sea-faring nations marched into the forests of Africa. Coast to coast, monkeys and apes lived distantly from humans, arboreal and largely herbivorous. In some places apes were sustainably hunted for meat, in others they were sacred and protected. Rumours reached the travellers of large man-like beasts – gorillas – lifting people into trees and suffocating them. There were stories of women carried off and raped. Tales of locals interbreeding with the apes. From the eighteenth century the British in particular cultivated their own mythology, tantalised by the apes' wild yet familiar appearance. In a mixture of observed behaviour and sentimental fantasy, they claimed the apes as competent tool-users who elaborately buried their dead (a claim similar to the latter is now popularly made of neanderthals). Imperial travellers were evidently intrigued by the 'civilising' potential in apes. They saw them, whether consciously or not, as part of the colonising project. The apes and the indigenous people likewise were considered junior relatives of the civilised European.

In what they did to the apes, imperial nations exhibited the attitudes they held towards the people they found in new lands. In the eighteenth century there was no clear consensus on humanity being a single thing, of all people belonging to the same species. Colonisers killed the apes, pitied them as children, and exported them for display. Thomas Belt, a nineteenth century naturalist, said there was 'something extremely disgusting in the idea of eating, what appears, when skinned and dressed, so like a child.' The apparently expressive eyes and mouths of the chimpanzee in particular, an animal which regularly stands and walks on two legs, encouraged the British to pity them, even partly to empathise with them – the shape of the face and head were broadly comparable with humans' – but did not deter their hunting.

Animal curios were brought back across the sea at the same time as adventurers from Walter Raleigh to Charles Darwin were exporting 'wild' men from the new lands for public viewing. Chimps and orang utans became Victorian playthings, produced into 'aped' human versions. In English captivity they were made to eat with cutlery, sip breakfast tea, sleep in beds and drink fine wines. 'Jenny', an orang taken to London zoo, was the first non-human primate Darwin ever saw. Queen Victoria said of another orang at the same zoo that it was 'frightful, and painfully and disagreeably human.'

Zoos were statements, celebrations of human dominion over the natural world. The British public was informed and assured of their own success and superiority over remoter lands and their inhabitants by the exhibitions of caged animals and displays of exotic flora. The chaos of a world they did not know was measured, domesticated and arrayed. The zoo was a vital colonial performance machine. The first British zoo was established in 1826 by Dr Stamford Raffles – eponymous now in the biggest unbranched flower in the world, *Rafflesia*, found in Borneo and Sumatra and notorious for the stench and appearance of rotting flesh. Not just in zoos but in natural history museums an elaborate theatre was presented. Empire officials became rich off dead wild animals. At Entebbe in Uganda British officials took wild animals in lieu of taxes. The paternal empire's administration was turning over the wilderness of non-British lands. Taxidermists – in work that still can be seen in exhibitions across the world – designed dead animals in aggressive poses to testify to the strength of the conqueror. Hunters were advised to record the final expression of their prey, which could then be recreated, and if need be exaggerated, in the austere halls of Europe. In 1861 Paul du Chaillu displayed gorillas with bullet-wounds posthumously inserted into the front of the body, to effect the emblem of a direct confrontation and disguise the scene of the ape fleeing in panic and being shot from behind.

A key administrative step in the move towards national parks was the signing in London in 1900 of the Convention for the Preservation of Wild

Animals, Birds and Fish in Africa. The convention's purpose was 'saving from indiscriminate slaughter and insuring the preservation of the various forms of animal life which are either useful to man or are harmless.' A similar convention was soon applied to Malaya, where the orang utan lived. Increased levels of hunting had led officials to realise the wild animals as valuable in some sense, stock which they owned and which was decreasing at a disturbing rate. The National Park of the twentieth century and beyond grew out of this. The first Park was established in 1925 within the huge region at the time called Belgian Congo, later Zaire, presently split between the Democratic Republic of Congo (DRC) and Congo Brazzaville. In the past 200 years this region has witnessed incredible levels of concentrated atrocity, effects of which continue. It is also an area of European mythologising and the place where imperialism and natural history most disturbingly converge.

The creation of this 3,000 sq mile park came at the behest of Prince Albert I towards the end of Belgium's rule. His predecessor, King Leopold II, had earlier declared personal rights over the entire 'Congo Free State', running it between 1885 and 1908 (when the country was transferred to Belgium) as a private estate which he mined for rubber, gold, diamonds, timber, and cobalt. In the twenty-three years of his occupation, up to 10 million indigenous people are estimated to have died – no records were kept – with large numbers also receiving mutilations of the body, such as the cutting off of one or both hands. This particular practice – cutting off hands, recurrent in contemporary central African war – began when Belgian soldiers were instructed not to waste ammunition hunting animals. The solution to ensuring bullets were only used necessarily – that is, to kill a non-acquiescing slave – was to make the effect of each shot transparent in the form of a presented human hand. To circumvent this – to continue leisurely killing both animals and humans – the soldiers would take a hand from a still living slave for every animal shot.

Belgium's activities met with only exceptional critical reporting, such as that of the Irishman Roger Casement, who acted as British consul in the Congo Free State between 1903–04 and who later witnessed atrocities upon Amerindians in South America and who was eventually hanged by the British state for treason. The enabling strategies of atrocity practice, on a colonial scale, involved not seeing the victim as human and thus not seeing his or her suffering as capacious or relatable to oneself; an obliteration of empathy.

The general 'less than human' – i.e. 'less than us' – appraisal by invaders of indigenous people evidenced throughout the history of imperialism, and seen symbolically in Victorian Britain's creation of zoos and Natural History Museums, reaches a culmination in Belgium's rule of the Congo. The history of Belgian- and independent- Congo also demonstrates the sometimes tragic and disastrous opportunities that imperialism presents to science.

New ape species were identified in Belgian Congo in the twentieth century in the form of the mountain gorilla and the bonobo, the latter a significantly different species of chimpanzee. The common chimpanzee also lives in this area; it is the greatest concentration of apes in the world. Its having a decimated and recently enslaved local human population and an abundant biodiversity, including exceptional primate populations, and a vast mineral wealth, led to the immediate and sustained foreign exploitation of post-colonial Congo (Zaire, DRC). The area has enticed western imagination, featuring in entertainments from *Heart of Darkness* to *Gorillas in the Mist*, used as a dark zone of foreign romance and self-discovery that seems key to the whole imperial project.

The region in and around independent Congo continued to be exploited long after Belgian rule, playing a part in some of the most significant and disturbing events of the twentieth century. Uranium used in A-bombs over Japan was taken from its forests. In neighbouring Rwanda in the 1950s Belgian officials conducted phrenology tests – measuring people's heads – and issued ethnically specific ID cards publicly distinguishing the resident Hutu from Tutsi people, a significantly contributing factor in the several outbreaks of driven xenophobic genocide later in the century, in which over a million people were killed, as neighbour murdered neighbour in hand-to-hand combat, often with farming tools for weapons. It is now almost certainly established that the first case of HIV was contracted through the eating of chimpanzee meat sourced from the Congo basin and infected with the equivalent Simian Immunodeficiency (SIV) disease. Central Africa has since suffered as a geographic concentration of HIV and AIDS.

Zoonosis is the transfer of disease between close species. The racist symbolism of Victorian zoos and colonial gardens, which hinted at both anxiety and fascination over kinship with remote peoples and non-human primates, is replaced by the tragically real demonstration, in a country ravaged by atrocity, that humans and animals are made of the same stuff.

*

National Parks and Reserves occupy a considerable proportion of Africa, a huge swathe of continent which, if combined, might comprise its biggest country. They are lucrative, generating hundreds of millions of pounds annually. In some countries National Park revenue is among the highest sources of GNP. The question of the rights of indigenous people living within the virtual bounds of the park has been controversial, though less so today. That humans live within reserves is something that has even been exploited, with foreign groups led on tours of 'traditional' villages in wilderness parts of Africa and Asia and South America. Companies specialise in 'first contact' experiences, leading tourists, in unconsciously ritualistic colonial repetition, to fraught near-confrontations with groups allegedly isolated from and innocent of the 'outside world'.

In Borneo by the Kinabatangan river I stayed in a hut with several other tourists, led out to the forest to see snakes and primates. We saw gibbons, proboscis monkeys, macaques, langurs. Several of us splintered and waded chin-deep through swamp, passports aloft in our outstretched hands, hoping for some danger. In the evening, desperate for a more immediate kind of encounter, I crept behind a young python we heard splashing in a pool. I was stunned as it leapt towards my chest, captive to its mechanical elegance and sinuous power, the flat purposiveness of its eyes in choosing me out.

One morning, the boat's engine cut; our guide shouted 'orang' and we made for the river bank. For the next forty minutes we watched three docile, passive, uninterested orangs dribbling leaves down the trees above us.

The experience was as contrived as 'first contact' (only the orangs were not getting paid). Apart from the thin fringe around the river, the forest had been decimated, replaced by row after row of palm-trees harvested for oil. Commercial habitat destruction – removing forest for timber or cash crops – has killed a far greater number of apes than hunting ever did. The mountain gorilla and the orang utan are almost extinct. They have also been slaughtered by mild human diseases to which they have no immunity, such as the common cold. In Rwanda and Uganda and the far-eastern DRC tourists pay between $400 and $750, take a health test, sign a declaration of well-being and are sprayed by disinfectant before finally being led up a hill and shown the gorillas.

The orangs that we saw, and who might have been expecting us such was their nonchalance, were most likely fed and handled by the guides, certainly monitored and encouraged to remain in the one area, contrary to their instincts. After observing them we returned to our huts in the clearing, damp mattresses draped in netting on the floor. There was a flooded walkway, a small sand football pitch, a makeshift bar. The environment was playful, staged; the animals were already caught, our awe of explorers was being indulged, as was the master-servant relationship of the client and his guide, again ritualistically repeating colonial clichés. I had come to Borneo to see orangs, to have an adventure, but also to see my brother, who lived near here, and whose savage beating and subsequent MRI scans had shocked me into a more visceral confrontation with the tactile, impressionable timbre of our own inner lives. The idea that someone may place a hand inside your head.

Flying to see my brother, I was window-side of an ex-soldier who enjoyed crossword puzzles and whose legs were paralysed. I was afraid of getting up and going to the toilet. We flew over the desert where he had been wounded. His daughter, a midwife, had saved up flyer-points so he could visit her, and he had had to take a three hour taxi-ride to reach the airport. It sounds redundant and self-evident, but I find it distressing to think that someone's identity – the way that they are – can be irrevocably changed by a too hard contact on the body. With head-wounds, the way that somebody thinks can be changed on at least two levels: their picture of the world may now be different because of something they have learned, and their psychological substance – from memory recall to temperament – may be altered due to neuronal damage, a change in the composition of what they think with. When I was taken to see half-wild orangs on the riverbank, what I was supposed to be feeling, I was told, was a wonderful sense of fraternity; instead I was picturing the melodramatic image of my brother going about his life two-dimensionally, with a flat surface of face concealing nothing.

The unresolvable question of the emergence of consciousness is at the heart of our interest in primates, and has historically featured in naïve and ignorant curiosity on the part of conquering nations, looking newly upon people that were different from themselves, wondering how human were these others. The modern story of non-human primates is a minor narrative within the history of European powers colonising other parts of the world from the fifteenth century onwards. In hunting, collecting, fetishising, and eradicating, colonisers did to the ape what they did to the people they encountered. The European-led installation of National Parks in ex-colonial regions, and their great popularity today, is partly a strange and idealised rendering of historical European activity. Apes are shocking reminders of a racism that questioned the humanity of foreign people. They also exist as representations of a recent stage in human lineage, information that generally, as a defensive species, we still do not know what to do with. I remember the completely irrational worry I had, after seeing the orangs, about their self-sufficiency, as if they somehow required benevolent human minding. Of course the worry should have been inverted: without humans they would flourish. But these identities are metaphorical, they are made from outside of the apes, hoisted onto them from solipsistic or speciesist humans. As all animals do, apes exist firstly as themselves. It is impossible to move clear of the suspicion that all human observation of apes is partly or largely really human self-commentary in lazily sublimated form. When we look at the details of ape behaviour we are amazed at ourselves. We are thunderstruck by the complexity of human society and the unfathomable subtlety of mind. In the ape, we might think, showing a dearth of imagination, is the seed of all of our unfolding.

In 1999 the journalist Ed Hooper travelled with the evolutionary-biologist Bill Hamilton to the DRC, determined to collect, in bonobo feces, proof that HIV had in fact arisen through medical use of contaminated bonobo kidney cells. Both men were entranced by the exotic and perilous journey, the dangerous thrill of entering a tropical war-zone. Hamilton took the journey again months later, naïve, romantic, hiking in ill-health, swindled out of sums of money by taxi-drivers. He contracted malaria, and died from a blood vessel ruptured in the course of his self-medicating.

Hamilton had a famously programmatic vision of human behaviour and life itself, popularised by his colleague Richard Dawkins in *The Selfish Gene* (1976). Hamilton devised equations calculating the utility of selfless actions performed for the benefit of relatives, the hypothesis being that life plays out ultimately in the interest of genes and not individuals. This de-humanised perspective, where the exceptional sanctity of human life is apparently discarded, seemed to open a dangerous moral vacuum, even to goad the state of terrible affectlessness in which people might kill each other.

The imaginative self-distancing of evolutionary-biologists in the last forty years or so, since the advent of the movement going by the now rarely used term sociobiology, has produced a canon of work investigating life through a celebratory humility. Their impossible aim has been to narrate life in its spatial and temporal fullness, and to be only minimally obstructed by the deceptive primacy of human personality and ego. Building on the work of pioneers like Charles Darwin and Alfred Russell Wallace – scientists whose field-work was enabled by empire – modern evolutionary-biologists are accused of stripping social and mental life to a rudimentary level, where actions have only invisible meaning and in theory anything may be done without culpability and the obligation of considering effect; essentially, of making life as cheap as it is in war. But shouldn't the essential instruction of evolutionary-biology be empathy? As it states, all life arises from a single and common originating point. Every organic thing is a unique extension of a temporary and unitary radiation. Life is mysterious, once, and whole.

There are no shortage of details we might find intriguing or evocative regarding the lives of apes. There are close mother-infant ties in at least the first three years across all apes – orang mothers teach their children for nine years; adult male gorillas periodically go on lone exile voyages of up to several months; bonobo chimpanzees are not afraid of bodies of water, as other apes are, seem to enjoy and are adept at standing on two legs, and have nervous sensibilities: they are known to cower at herds of passing oxen. (During the bombing of Munich in WWII, the bonobos and chimpanzees held in Hellabrunn zoo endured markedly different fates: all of the chimpanzees survived, while none of the bonobos did, their hearts arrested from the impact of the sound.) Bonobos and chimpanzees are capable of empathy, putting themselves in the mind of another. The primatologist Frans de Waal reports seeing a wounded bonobo affect a limp *only* when in view of the ape that attacked it, and another temporarily obscuring the anxious expression on its face so as to dissuade its pursuer. Orangs and chimpanzees can experience elements of the mirror stage of early psychological development. Bononos are so fascinated by reflected images of themselves they study shards of glass, tin, even their own urine-puddles in zoo enclosures. Chimpanzees are the only species of mammal, after humans, to engage in intra-species warfare, hunting in packs and indulging in cannibalism. And in an unsettling echo of two of the principle beliefs still of western thought – that the history of life is of an ascension to civilized man, and that meaningful life will rise from a dead body – Sarah Blaffer Hrdy observes a gorilla will carry its dead child for several days – until there is nothing left but a strip of skin – because the energy expended in doing this is so little as to be evolutionarily worthwhile: once in every thousandth instant the infant will wake.

Sources and Further Reading

Thomas Belt, *The Naturalist in Nicaragua* (John Murray, 1874)

Bill Hamilton, *Narrow Roads of Gene Land* Vol.1 (W.H. Freeman, 1997)

Sarah Blaffer Hrdy, *Mothers and Others* (Vintage, 2000)

Ed Hooper, *The River: A Journey Back to the Source of HIV and Aids* (Penguin 1999)

Harriet Ritvo, *The Animal Estate* (Harvard University Press, 1987)

Ullica Segerstrale, *Nature's Oracle: The Life and Work of W.D. Hamilton* (Oxford University Press, 2013)

Frans de Waal, *Peacemaking Among Primates* (Harvard University Press, 1990)

Matthew Sweeney

The Other Bible

It took them until 2073 to meet us,
to land in a flurry of flashing lights
on the outskirts of Adelaide, their
cruciform-shaped craft glowing
lemon yellow, and emitting a low
music that brought dogs barking.

The police arrived too, blaring and
shouting into phones that the army
must come. They ordered us all
to keep our distance, but the dogs
ignored this and stood around,
whimpering, till a door opened.

I inched forward but was pushed
back. I was still one of the closest
to the two tall figures who emerged –
giraffe tall, with dog faces – and
the silence around us was celestial.
Even the police became Zen monks.

So smart of them not to choose
America, I reflected, and a firm
thought-command drew me forward,
the police backing away, till I stood
in front of the two tall figures,
hand held out, but they ignored this.

Instead, tendons came from their
bellies which curled round my head,
and they thought-spoke to me in
unison, saying they came in peace
from planet *Illyos*. I glanced around
and verbalised a welcome, which was

echoed loudly. Then they conveyed
to me they wanted to present an
offering, and something very like
a book, in a fantastic edition, came
floating out of the craft, and one of
the two directed it into my hands.

Hieroglyphs, was what occurred to me,
picture stories, weird, futuristic ones –
a tall dog-faced figure with a yellow
cruciform glowing above his head,
flying through space, hauling a horde
of airborne devotees to a yellow valley

in a pleasant world that wasn't ours —
it had above it a faint lavender sky.
I saw no more, except it was their past.
They registered this, re-entered their
craft, which glowed yellow, and took
off as three army vehicles whizzed up.

The Ghost

can go through walls, if he wants to
but he does it seldom. He prefers
to adhere to the limits he had before,
as he'd like to be alive again, playing
golf at Ballybunion, making love to his
girlfriend, cooking *choucroute* with
roast, pre-marinated, loin of pork,
and opening a *Côtes du Rhône Villages*.
But the mountains will fall in the sea
before that can happen, so he drifts
about over the heads of the people
he cared for, occasionally letting them
glimpse him but not be sure they did.

Sometimes he releases a faint, garlic
smell, other times he emits an almost
musical hum, although he could never
sing. Contrary to hearsay, he favours
the day over the night, as the moon
gives him the creeps, even now, while
the sun reminds him of bodily warmth.
Body...! What he'd give to get his own
back, the way it was when he was twenty,
but what has he to give? A spurious aura
that no one believes in? Anyway, he's
here and he's not here, and he knows
he's not wanted but he's staying on.

New York

1

I kept glimpsing Lou
Reed's ghost as I roamed
Manhattan – there he
was on street corners,
in every sportsbar. I
heard snatches of his
songs on the urban wind.
It was the middle of
a perfect, perfect day.

2

If only time machines
weren't so expensive,
or had such side-effects,
I'd go back to drink red
wine with Frank O'Hara –
I'm sure we'd find one
we both liked. I'm less
sure he'd like this, but
there's always a chance.

3

At MOMA I stood for
ages in front of Magritte's
Daring Sleeper, the baldie
under the brown blanket
in the tigerskin-patterned
box, the apple, candle,
bird, blue bow, hairbrush,
hand-mirror embedded in
the higgledy-piggledy gravestone before the overcast sky.
I stared, remembering it all.

4

I tried to take a taxi to the
Chelsea Hotel but the cabbie
went on a wide detour in
bad traffic, and when I saw
I was back in Midtown, I
hopped out and slunk off
to my small, unsung hotel.

5

In West Village a pair of
bums approached – one with
a wilted flower in his button-
hole. They watched a long,
black car pull in, allowing
the driver to jump out and
buy an apple. I heard
one bum say to the other
Oh, man, there's our limo.

6

In Bleeker Street I found
the world's best cheese-
shop (well, the oldest in
New York) and coolest
Italian deli, and I bought
designer pasta, then took
my red eye and sore toe to
the Slaughtered Lamb pub.

7

On West 4th Street I had
a hell of nerve, and stood
in front of Dylan's old flat,
where he invited someone to
please crawl out her window.
Yeah… I wanted to photo
-graph it but a sex-shop
downstairs intervened.

8

At the side of Washington
Square was the dog-run.
From all sides dogs on leads
made for it, to be set free
and allowed to run in packs,
barking – except for the Afghan
who sat on the bench with his
mistress, observing everything.

9

In Union Square's Farmers'
Market, I drank goat's-milk
yoghurt, then followed closely
three chess games on the street-
side. I'd have lost each one.

10

In a Mexican Restaurant
in East Village I ate monkfish
with molé and fried, green
bananas, also slow-roasted
pork with green sauce. I drank
three margaritas, and some
Argentinian red wine.
A sombrero floated down
and landed on my head.

11

Back in Hell's Kitchen I
wandered down 9th Avenue
to Petland, and bought a
frondy thing for Derek, my
goldfish, then crossed to the
Amish deli for watermelon juice.

12

In JFK's Security, where the
black guys in uniform made me
laugh, I launched five plastic
trays through the screener –
one with my boots, one my
belt and jacket, and bag of
little bottles, one my new
mini i-Pad, the last two with
my rucksacks, big and small.

Jenni Fagan

Parliament

He was an old man with claws for hands.

That wasn't why you called him the bird man, you called him that because he fed the crows in Princes Street Gardens. His fingernails were yellow, curved things. The bird man was a friend of the father and son.

The father was eighty-seven and the son was sixty-three. Early morning just before 6am, they'd walk through the train departures hall (which had a stained glass dome ceiling) and head for their usual table in the food court.

Breakfast was always the same. They would both order a bacon/egg muffin and large cups of tea. They'd sit on red plastic chairs and take their hats off and wait for the day to start.

Your area was front-of-house, and your early shift started at 5.30am. You had to wipe down tables, sweep the floor, mop, empty bins. Then you'd refill the condiments area with skinny brown and white sugar sachets, salt, pepper and little plastic cups of milk or cream.

At the back a small raised area had two tables and you had to go up there to clean as well. It was where the rent boys would always sit (just finished their night shift) and you'd put down clean disposable ashtrays made of green tin. They'd be jittery on speed come downs and they'd chain smoke until the coffee percolator gurgled to life. They didn't eat. They just drank a lot of coffee and jiggled their legs around.

Then there was the bird man. He would usually come in after 6am (his familiar bird shuffle – a fragile gait) and he'd look over to see if you were there (you were the only one who'd serve him) but if it was just Charles he'd leave again. Charlie's designated area was the fryers, coffee machine and till. You were meant to be strictly front-of-house but you broke that rule anytime the bird man came in. That was why you and fat Charles were at war.

- Next time the tramp comes in *don't* serve him.

- I'll serve who I want, fatso.

Charles's face would go all blotchy then and he'd shake a wee bit like he wanted to dunk your head (repeatedly) in the hot fat fryer.

- We don't serve homeless people, it's company policy.

- That's a fucking stupid policy.

- Do you want to make a complaint to the people who make company policy?

- All I'm saying is – everyone deserves a cup of tea.

- No, *everyone* does not, watch your step, I could get you fired you know, really easily!

You served the bird man a cup of tea and he shuffled away quietly. You did not look Charles in the eye but you could feel rage emanating from him like a fever. It seemed a good time to go out back (by the big bins) and smoke a few roll-ups.

Roll-ups made from dog ends always tasted like shit but it was something you had to resort to a lot in the homeless accommodation. You liked to think of it as a kind of recycling. You were not the only one who did it (unpicking the end of cigarettes to roll new ones) and they always made your throat burn.

You also always nicked your toilet roll from work and hand-wash for when you ran out of shampoo. In the burger bar you got one meal per shift, and a snack at your other break. On your days off you often made a meal from pasta shells and chicken soup. You were so pleased with yourself when you concocted that one. It was cheap and easy, and it tasted better with pepper in it.

Charles didn't know about that and he didn't know you used to sleep rough. It's not something you told people but you especially didn't want him to find out because it would only fuel his superiority complex.

- I got promoted!

He sneered one morning and right enough, there it was – a shiny Assistant Manager's badge with Charles St Clair written on it. Some new guy was frying burgers. You put your bag down as a feeling of dread overcame you. Charles had spent the last six months climbing up the bosses rectum/massaging his sweaty ball sacks. Evidently it had paid off.

- You have to do what I say now, he'd said.

- No, I fucking don't.

YES, actually – you fucking do!

Charles got worse the more you were around him. You noticed his hairless arms – how he masticated with his mouth open so you could see his saliva and food – and he often pointed chips at people when he was talking. He still called his old dear mummy.

Then one morning, he decided to be nice to you.

- You can take a break, read a paper and have a smoke behind the pillar out there, nobody will see you. It's got to be better than standing out back by the bins!

So you did and that's where you were (sitting with your doc boots up on a chair) reading a paper and having a smoke – when the manager came around the corner.

- What do you think you're doing? he'd asked.

- Charles said I could take a break here.

No I did not! Nobody is allowed to take a break *in-front-of-customers*!

You said to take a break *front-of-house* – Charles, that's what you said!

- I would *never* say that.

The boss looked at Charles then he looked at your feet, and your nose stud, and your cigarette still burning in the ashtray.

- You're fired, he said.

- Fucking, fine!

Charles visibly glowed as you were marched off the food court. When you looked back the father and the son gave you a wee wave and you waved back and wondered who'd give the bird man his cup of tea now.

That week you tried to find another shit job so you could pay your rent. The thing was – you had no qualifications, no references, and you'd left school at fifteen. If you didn't pay your rent you'd be made homeless again (homeless accommodation is shit like that) so eventually you had to do something you'd never done before.

You went to the dole office for the first time in your life.

The DSS building at Castle Terrace was grey and concrete and ugly as shit. Inside there were two queues and you had to fill out a form and hand it through a window. Then you had to join another queue to get a green ticket.

You stood in the queue for the machine that dispensed tickets and it reminded you of the deli counter but a lot less friendly. Eventually it was your turn and the little bit of card slid out like a tongue and written on it was the number 143.

A security man pointed – gesturing that you should go into the main room next door. You didn't want to go in there. It was a large room and the interview spaces were separated by plastic barriers so you (the scum) could not attack them (the benefits advisors).

The first time you walked in to the waiting area, a woman with ginger hair head-butted a plastic screen. She shouted a lot, saying things like – she was going to fucking murder someone and she didn't give a fuck who saw her do it. You sidled into a corner seat and tried not to have a panic attack and you just knew the jakeys and wierdos would gravitate your way.

They did.

A light on the wall lit up with numbers so each person would know when it was their turn. You chewed all your nails down, and your skin felt prickly, and you tried not to make eye contact with anyone. A year or so later your number lit up. You walked into a tiny room where a woman with a face like a cunt told you she was going to process your claim.

- Why were you fired?

- I was told I could take a break by one of the staff but he lied to get me in trouble.

- That's *not* what he said.

- Well, that *is* what happened.

- Why are you trying to claim housing benefit, when you are – only sixteen?

- I need to pay rent at my homeless accommodation.

- You should have thought of that before you left your parents house.

- I was in a kids home, I don't have parents.

- That's *not* our problem.

You were shocked by that, and embarrassed. You'd never said it was her problem, and a blush stained your cheeks because you were not there for charity. You sat up straight and tried to act like a grown up.

- If I can't pay rent I'll lose the bedsit.

- Why don't you live with someone else in your family?

You wished you'd brought one of the support workers along with you (they'd told you it might be difficult) but you didn't think it'd be so stickily humiliating.

- I've just left care.

- So, now you think you're owed a handout?

You wanted to cry because you didn't have anyone to stay with and you didn't want to sleep rough again and you were so fucking uneasy, so crippled by fear, and flashbacks, and panic attacks that you could barely function anyway.

That night you walked back into Casey Jones and asked to see your boss.

- Can I see Calvin?

- What do you want to see Calvin for?

Charles had demanded this while glancing at your tits. You were wearing a tight t-shirt and a hooded coat made of big coloured velvet squares. You were very stoned and it was helping you to stay focused.

- I want my job back.

- Not likely, he'd said.

- Calvin, you shouted.

Calvin emerged from his office and punched in the pin code so the door would open to let you through.

- I really need this job, I'm *really* sorry about taking a break in front of the customers.

As you said the words you felt unclean and like your ancestors were rolling over in their graves and you could tell Calvin really liked that.

- What about the nose stud? he'd asked.

- I can't take it out. It's stuck.

- You could cover it with a plaster, for hygiene purposes.

- Okay.

- Can I ask you something? he'd said.

- Aye.

- Do you like my tight buns?

He'd stood up and turned around and showed you his arse in his tight black trousers and you'd thought that your face could not possibly go any more red.

- Well?

- I, eh, I don't, eh, I dinnae ken.

You were panicking then and he seemed to like that too.

- Okay. You need to cover the nose stud, and you'll have to buy a pair of proper shoes, you can't wear Doc boots.

You nodded and reasoned that he'd forget about your boots eventually (you weren't giving them up) and maybe you could find a flat nose stud so you could just dab foundation over it.

- Can I tell you something, in confidence? he asked.

You'd wondered what it was about you that made people tell you things that you wished they'd never told you, and braced yourself – it was lucky you did.

- I killed someone once, in Australia, before I left, killed him stone dead.

You didn't know what to say and you had never met an Australian before but you didn't fucking like this one. You said nothing and he stared at you for a long, long time.

- One more chance then, and by the way – loosen up, I don't fucking fancy you anyway.

Monday was your first day back. You began at 5.30am and would work until 2pm – on early shifts for a fortnight. You slapped off your alarm at 5am and reached for the dregs of a bong. Your boyfriend was sleeping but you woke him up and shagged him. Then you finished the bong. It took a minute to dress in your uniform (dicky bow tie, thick v-neck jumper, shirt, polyester skirt which was way too big) and it was back in business again.

You got in early and Charles was on the till, counting out the day's float. He slammed the drawer shut when he saw you approaching. You went downstairs, hung up your jacket, took the mop out the front, mopped the floors, cleaned the tables, emptied the bins, put down disposable ashtrays.

- What's that? Charlie glared at your nose stud.

- I'll put a plaster over it, you'd said.

- Take it fucking out.

- No. Calvin said I could put a plaster over it.

- Well, he's not here right now, is he?

The father and the son were sitting together. They were waiting for the griddle to heat up for their burgers and eggs to go on. The son was smaller than the father (his face just as lined) and he wore his usual outfit – brown trousers, old coat (buttoned up) jumper underneath. The son had a tweed hat with a fisherman's hook in it. The father dressed the same except his hat had a wide band around it, and he wore a scarf.

- How are you both today?

They smiled and they liked it when you chatted and they always told you their news.

- Not bad, nice to see you back. Our window's still broken!

- Who broke it again?

- Local lads, they think we are, you know!

The son made an old fashioned gesture with his hand because he didn't want to say the word gay. The father glanced over to the other corner of the food court where the rent boys were chatting quietly.

- Have you seen the bird man in this last week?

- Aye, he's alright, he'll be glad to see you back though. Did you know he was once manager of the most expensive hotel in town? Aye. One time a Japanese princess was staying in the penthouse, and a sniper had been paid tae assassinate her. He was hiding out with a gun, on Jenners' roof!

- He missed though ay, or he fell off the roof or something. She sent a thank you to him (when he was still manager) by way of a Fabergé egg!

The son finished the story. Behind you the new guy was frying their burgers now and cracking eggs onto the hot plate.

- Why did he not keep his job? you asked.

- Just couldn't go back one day, not to the job, not even to a room with a bed, or a door. He couldn't do it anymore so he didn't, the son said.

You totally understood.

Charles was on the phone to someone. You cleaned the rest of the tables, laid out a few more ashtrays.

- He layers his clothes you know, the father said.

- How'd you mean?

- The top layer is cleaner, it doesnae smell so much, so he takes it off, puts it down at the bottom, moves everything up one. It takes ages. He does it once a week in the public toilet. He shaves there unnaw, or in the wing mirrors of cars before everyone else gets up.

Something about that made you want to cry. You imagined the bird man standing in front of the wing mirror of a car with his razor. In those early hours the only sound would be birds, or silence, or some domestic fight far away somewhere, or even just drunks on their way home.

There was still time to take a break before Casey Jones opened to the public and there was no sign of the bird man yet so you went out back by the bins. You lit a smoke and stared out over the underground car park. Behind the bins there was an entrance to the catacombs. It was a big room with brick walls that had been spray painted with graffiti. It had lots of rubble, and rubbish, and smashed bottles on the floor.

Calvin showed you that room on your first day (training) and told you that it was an entrance to the catacombs. He told you the catacombs ran right under the city and if you walked in to them you'd never make it back out.

Casey Jones was the only part of the railway station that still had an open entrance into the catacombs and it was not common knowledge – but the staff knew about it. They had to be warned. It was train station policy. Charles reckoned it was because they lost a cleaner or two in there one night.

Sometimes you stuck one foot into the catacomb, and just stood there. You supposed some people might sleep in there, underneath the city, and you wondered why the council had not blocked the entrance off.

Out by the bins you had strange thoughts. You'd smoke until you were dizzy and wonder if this was life. Sometimes you'd imagine a stranger in a suit striding past the bin area. He'd see you, and walk right over, haul your skirt up and fuck you against the wall. You thought of that a lot but it didn't make sense because you hated suits, and casual sex. The human brain was more and more clearly – not a place of logic.

Back in the food court you felt pale under the hot lights and your jumper was jaggy and the bow tie bugged you. Later on you knew that men would leave you little notes on tables with their numbers on them and you would put them in the bin.

Out in the departures waiting room the sunlight was bright so the stained glass roof cast colours on the tiled floor. It was a beautiful room, and you would have liked to live there but without the pigeons or departures board. Just then the bird man shuffled in – toward the food court and you had a jolt of electricity like somehow your life up until now had been leading to this. The father and son watched as the bird man approached, and the rent boys (up in their corner) were lighting fresh cigarettes.

- Serve him and you're sacked for good this time!
- Calvin won't fire me, not this time.
- Do you want to test that out do you?
- Aye.

A single crow walked in the front entrance. It walked in, there was no mistaking it. It had its hands behind its back and it walked around as if it was deep in thought. Three more walked in behind it and one of them cocked its head and its wee black eye stared right at you.

- It's a braw morning, the father said.
- It is that, you said.

Out in the departures lounge more crows flew in, they perched on plastic chairs, and on window ledges, and above doors. One sat on the led board – which announced the 6am to Colchester was DELAYED.

- The council still didnae replace our window, the father said.

The son nodded and you nodded.

- I could help you write a letter.

You didn't know why you were offering, seeing as you could barely write and your spelling was terrible.

More crows ventured into the food court, they were everywhere now and they looked like police officers, bent over – spread out across a big park looking for murder clues. The bird man was there, in front of you then and the clock on the wall read 5.59am exactly.

Right at the entrance to the food court, three crows sat, high above the others, like they were deciding something.

Nobody said a word.

The hot water button was a bit sticky so you wiped it, then poured boiling water over a tea bag. You added milk, and fixed a lid on the styrofoam cup. You grabbed four sugars and a little plastic strip with a hole in the end that was meant to pass for a spoon.

It took an effort to squeeze around Charles. You put the tea down in front of the bird man, he reached out and took it, his black eyes glancing away.

- You're fired.

Charles said it quietly to you then he leaned over the counter and shouted at the bird man.

- If you come back here tomorrow – I'll call the police. You disgust me! You STINK!

The air was warm with the smell of frying fat and fresh percolated coffee and the rent boys had disappeared. You watched the bird man shuffle away, his tatty old mac was shredded at the bottom, just tatters hanging there. His ripped carrier bags were rammed full of stuff, and his leather shoes were so worn and brown they seemed like they'd become his actual feet.

- You really shouldnae talk to him like that, the father said.

- Shut up, you old idiot!

Crows alighted on every table, black eyes, beaks, gnarled claws, caw-caw-caw-caw-caw-caw and the bird man (right out there under the glass dome) was *not* a man then and your ancestors were glad.

Ryan Van Winkle

Dress

Mermaid-like with promised stones
of silk organza rosettes, strapless blue
and sunset pink. The cake round,

not square, four tiers, no columns, no masts
and strawberries please
for the filling. Like blood

at the corners of our mouths, filling
spilled from my captive hand
and onto your dress, like a kiss

smeared ugly on a cheek. Punctured
gasps as if Aunt Barbara had fallen
on her hip and I rushing for a cloth –

someone shouting baking soda,
someone shouting salt. Imagine
the cost of the wreckage, and you

(I should have known), hushed and
pushed us away like clouds, said no, said
this is beginning.

Flag

I know you have a lot on your list
and that list has been a flag you have flown
across plains and prairies, down little state roads
down white and green and black mountains
down to the league games, to the ovens when fire
was high in the sky, so many nights going down
before you'll take time to white the flag, rest.

If you point gold
at the sky what
do you think will fall
*

If I think of New York bagels
I am not here and still
I am not there saying 'I used to have no walls.'
I was a young Barcelona growing
steeples, raining sand, I knew what I meant
when I pointed us
at the map
*

I am headed in a circle, a circle but a little to the left. Still, worth tapping
the brakes, still worth flashing the lights to say, 'Slow down
there is a black & white approaching.' You can't see it but everybody knows
Barcelona is not famous for a castle. Barcelona will never be famous
for a Hard Rock Cafe I cried to enter, some marathon
route some high school friend ran, round about 7 o'clock, just for an hour
while we napped, slept poorly, knowing we might never come back, forgetting
Barcelona for years until some kid I used to know well, who ran
part of a marathon route died in his sleep and we were awoken still
in Barcelona.
*

So long as there is road
there will be cassettes
made for the road
*

If Mostar is still there
I will be there at night
If the bridge stands
there will be a card
to an address I forget
*

So long as there is root
fathers will keep planting

Caves

The stalactite growing down,
the pond drying and the river mute,
choked by ice and my grandfather, under
all that dirt, hiding his final thoughts;
stolen, clear-eyed marbles I buried
in his backyard and never found again.

Victoria E. Price

A Cycle of History Plays for Scotland: Rona Munro's *The James Plays*

At the 2014 Edinburgh International Festival the National Theatre of Scotland (NTS) presented a new cycle of history plays focusing on three generations of Stewart Kings who ruled Scotland in the fifteenth century. This trilogy of histories, *The James Plays*, explores the lives of James I, James II and James III and brings to our attention a little-known period in Scottish history. The three plays have been written by acclaimed playwright Rona Munro and are centrally concerned with questions of Scottish history and Scottish identity; they directly engage in the history, development and forging of a nation, asking provocative questions about that nation's past and its future. It is apt that this dynastical trilogy, arguably one of the most exciting and ambitious theatrical projects to be undertaken in Scotland in recent years, was first staged in a historic year, premièring just a month before the Independence referendum.

Described by NTS as 'epic historical theatre for remarkable times',[1] the trilogy is directed by NTS Artistic Director Laurie Sansom in a co-production with Edinburgh International Festival (EIF) and the National Theatre of Great Britain – strikingly, this production marks the first time the two national theatres have collaborated (following its EIF run it transferred to the Olivier Theatre at the National Theatre in London).[2] Its ensemble cast of twenty includes James McArdle, Andrew Rothney, Jamie Sives, *Taggart* star Blythe Duff and Sofie Gråbøl from the popular Danish TV series *The Killing*.

The trilogy begins with *James I: The Key Will Keep The Lock*, which tells the story of a man who has spent eighteen years of his life as a prisoner of the English and who arrives home to take up his crown in a deeply divided Scotland, with an English bride by his side. *James II: Day of the Innocents* depicts a king crowned at the age of eight, trapped as a pawn in the power games of the country's most powerful families. This boy-king finds he must grow up quickly and fight the feuding nobles if he wants to hold onto his monarchical position and secure the realm. *James III: The True Mirror*, the final instalment of Munro's trilogy, portrays the charismatic, ambitious and wayward king whose queen, Margaret of Denmark (played by Gråbøl) must intercede with his subjects in order to avoid civil war and regicide and ensure the stability of his country. Although individually each play presents a distinct and unique story of a fifteenth-century monarch as he struggles to hold onto his fragile crown, taken collectively *The James Plays* offers a poignant consideration of issues such as national identity and the governance of Scotland as a nation. As such, the trilogy is very timely and politically charged, examining urgent questions of how to run a country and organise a nation.

But why focus on this rarely explored period of history? Why present a set of plays about medieval history in the lead up to the referendum? A trio of history plays notably set *before* the Union of Scotland and England, *The James Plays* becomes a really great vehicle for thinking through the political concerns of the present. The trilogy becomes a lens through which to think about the forging of a nation, inviting audiences to probe some of the past events that have led to the current political moment and to think about the future of that nation, its governance and organisation.

Munro is not, of course, the only playwright to turn to the past, and to the history play in particular, as a means of examining the political present. One thinks here of Shakespeare and the famous example of *Richard II*. When Shakespeare wrote about the medieval reign of Richard II, he assuredly saw the conflicts of that reign through the lens of the late sixteenth century: the play might be set in the medieval period but the English playwright could not conceal from audiences in his own time the contemporary relevance of the play, which is concerned with the theme of succession and what it is to be a king. Shakespeare was putting quill to parchment at a time when the ageing Elizabeth had no named successor and the proper extent of a monarch's power was a crucial, and unresolved, issue.

Shakespeare's dramatic representation of Richard II was largely intended as a criticism of Elizabeth's government and her actions. Of primary concern to the Crown was the deposition scene contained in the play: in all sixteenth-century printed texts the lines where Richard gives up his crown were omitted, the scene considered too inflammatory to print or stage. However, when Robert Devereux, the second Earl of Essex rebelled against Elizabeth in 1601, some of his followers persuaded Shakespeare's company, the Lord Chamberlain's Men, to put on a special performance of *Richard II* in an attempt to rally further support for their cause. Essex was disillusioned with Elizabeth's government and in particular with the court faction led by Sir Robert Cecil that was seeking to gain further influence at court. The historical story of Richard II seemed to provide a strategic and relatively safe means of commenting indirectly on this political situation. The production, though, aroused the concern of the authorities, with the scene of Richard's removal as king considered by many an act of sedition against the queen. The Lord Chamberlain's Men responded by claiming they had just been paid some money to put on an old play that had been written many years ago and had nothing to do with the Earl of Essex. They managed to wash their hands of the affair, but it was nevertheless a very dangerous brush with politics. This example reveals a clear attempt to use a history play to intervene politically in the present.

Shakespeare, of course, was writing during what has been hailed as the Golden Age for the history play. For the 1590s was the most important decade for the development of the history play; this was a time when the whole subject of England's past became dramatically fashionable. Other dramatists who turned to the past in order to reflect on the Tudor regime and Elizabeth's part within it include: Henry Chettle, Thomas Dekker, George Gascoigne, John Hayward, Thomas Heywood, Christopher Marlowe, Thomas Nashe, George Peele and Philip Webster, to name but a few. Many of these playwrights turned to the legendary events of the English history narrated by the Tudor chroniclers, Edward Hall and Raphael Holinshed for material they could (re-) examine and reshape. History was valued by humanist educationalists in the sixteenth century as a great teaching tool and a source of moral instruction, and so it is not surprising that many dramatists of the 1590s found in Hall's *The Union of the Two Noble and Illustre Famelies of Lancastre and York* (1548) and Holinshed's *Chronicles of England, Scotland and Ireland (*a second edition of this text was published in 1587) compelling lessons for the present.

The history play proved to be exceptionally popular with paying audiences during this decade. At a time when only fifteen to thirty per cent of the population was literate, theatre was a powerful medium of publication and the history play offered a chance for spectators to hear what playwrights thought about the topical issues of the day. Plays of national histories that depicted exciting events from the past (crises such as wars, usurpations, domestic rebellions and uprisings, changes of monarchy, invasions and foreign threats) could be employed to warn, to teach lessons, and/or to celebrate victories. Many operated to preserve the memory of past English heroes and by extension to inspire audiences to feelings of patriotism and loyalty to the crown. There is no doubt, though, that representations of the past could be interpreted more subversively, as a source of analogies to controversial contemporary events, as the example of *Richard II* has shown. To this end, Dominique Goy-Blanquet captures the significance of historical writing in the period when he calls it 'a double-edged weapon, as dangerous as it was powerful'.[3]

The high volume of playwrights experimenting in the 1590s with dramatising English history is not accidental. These are plays that offer very direct and demystified portrayals of power politics at work, with many playwrights simultaneously providing provocative comments upon the failings of those governing the nation. Their explorations of the relationships between those in political authority and the people can be seen to have been triggered by a national crisis – the Spanish Armada of 1588. The spate of history plays in the post-Armada period can therefore be interpreted as responding to this critical moment in the life of the nation, the plays themselves offering a vehicle through which audiences could debate national affairs and examine the complex inner workings of power.

Just as with the long tradition of English Chronicle plays, so too there has been a strong engagement with history in Scottish playwriting traditions. One period that has been especially striking for the Scottish stage's rich engagement with history is the 1970s and 80s. This treatment of historical material was in part due to the historiographical practices of the 1960s and 1970s – especially the work of Angus Calder, Christopher Hill, T.C. Smout and E.P. Thompson – which were concerned with exploring 'hidden history'.[4] The excavation, rediscovery and re-examination of Scottish history coincided with, what Ian Brown has termed a 'surge in Scottish self-awareness and developing self-confidence, typified culturally by a range of phenomena in the decade between 1963 and 1973', including the opening of the Traverse Theatre, the foundation of Scottish Opera and Scottish Ballet, and the establishment of the Scottish Society of Playwrights.[5] The rewriting of history taking place within much Scottish drama at this time was clearly part of a wider cultural process.

In 1996 Brown wrote an essay in which he explores how many Scottish dramatists have been 'plugged into history', noting that although the treatment of history before 1970 may have been generally sentimental and backward looking, since then its developing use has been concerned with the 'now' of Scotland, its identity and future.[6] And so it can be said that Rona Munro with her *The James Plays* is following in the footsteps of, for example, Hector MacMillan and John McGrath, who registered in their plays an awareness of how history can be adapted and manipulated for particular political agendas. Brown says of MacMillan's dramaturgy – with reference to *The Rising* (1973) and *The Royal Visit* (1974) – that he 'revisits history in order to reveal what is hidden within it, and, through questioning the ways in which it has been hidden, to examine the nature of contemporary power, political propaganda and manipulation of opinion'.[7] In *The Rising*, MacMillan provides his audience with an account of the betrayal of the Scottish Insurrection or Radical War of 1820. *The Royal Visit* focuses on Sir Walter Scott's political stage management of the royal visit of George IV to Edinburgh in 1822. In both plays MacMillan breaks with the sentimental tradition that had been identified on the Scottish stage prior to the 1970s and employs historical material in order to hold up a mirror to contemporary Scotland.

John McGrath, meanwhile, in *The Cheviot, the Stag and the Black, Black Oil* (1973) and other plays engaging with history – for example, *Little Red Hen* (1975) and *Joe's Drum* (1979) – visits the past in order to examine political myth and ultimately to reconstruct historical myths as motive for future action. McGrath and 7:84 (Scotland)'s *The Cheviot, the Stag and the Black, Black Oil* is undoubtedly the most influential Scottish history play of the late twentieth century. It draws on historical material over three centuries in order to present Scottish history, from the Highland Clearances to the 1970s discovery of North Sea oil, as marked by exploitation and struggle. *The Cheviot* fuses fact and fiction and draws on the oral storytelling traditions of the céilidh, which McGrath enriches with tropes such as the double-act and satirical sketch drawn from popular commercial forms. In production, the historical material was presented in dialogue with contemporary Scotland, the past being employed to explicate and comment on the present.

McGrath also addressed other aspects of Scottish history elsewhere in his playwriting: social and industrial unrest in early twentieth-century Glasgow (the Red Clydeside period) and the Glasgow Marxist John MacLean's life are explored in *The Game's a Bogey* (1974); working-class women's exploitation in post-war Britain is the focus of *Little Red Hen* (1975); and, Scottish nationalism's history is dealt with in *Border Warfare* (1989).[8] Indeed, although the dominant subject matter of history plays in this period focuses on working-class men, many playwrights did choose to concentrate on a larger range of historical contexts. Sue Glover, for example, in her 1988 play *The Straw Chair* deals with questions of male power and political corruption in eighteenth-century Scotland as an Edinburgh minister and his new wife arrive on St Kilda to find Lady Rachel in effect exiled there by order of her husband, the Lord Advocate, in order to prevent her revealing his political duplicity and treason. Liz Lochhead's *Mary Queen of Scots Got Her Head Chopped Off* (1987) explores the myths of Mary and her cousin Elizabeth I, and examines the nature of Scottishness, its oppositions and contradictions. Whether in plays that focus on individuals or in those that concentrate on larger historical perspectives, playwrights in this period exhibit a very imaginative approach to history. They bring the past to the stage in order to re-examine the very concept and nature of both Scotland and history. All the plays from the 1970s and 80s discussed here illustrate how history can be reinterpreted and combined with contemporary comment in order to intervene politically in the present. Above all, these plays question notions of the 'facts of history'.

During the 1990s, there was arguably a move away from both plays and the past, due in part to a postmodern and/or postdramatic shift away from narrative in favour of devised collaborative performance. As David Archibald has observed:

Glasgow's Tramway, which opened in 1988, and the Edinburgh International Festival have both played an important role in programming post-dramatic theatre in recent years. Companies like La Fura del Baus, Forced Entertainment and Goat Island have regularly visited Scotland over the last two decades and influenced theatre-makers, who have moved away from traditional narrative-based theatre. Of course, venues like Edinburgh's Traverse, which describes itself as 'Scotland's new writing theatre', still produces and stages many new plays, but plays in Scotland overall are being produced in decreasing numbers: noticeably Glasgow's The Arches, one of Scotland's most dynamic theatre venues, rarely programmes traditional text-based plays.[9] Archibald goes onto note there is a tendency for post-dramatic theatre to limit its engagement with the past to relatively recent events, in contrast to the more traditional work of playwrights who draw more widely on the past.

In recent years, though, there has been a renewed return to and re-engagement with history in the Scottish theatrical landscape, with plays such as David Harrower's *Blackbird* (2005), Gregory Burke's *Black Watch* (2006), Douglas Maxwell's *The Ballad of James II* (2007), Munro's *The Last Witch* (2009), and Alistair Beaton's *Caledonia* (2010), treating historical events and themes as serious creative and dramatic discourse and at the same time addressing both historical interpretation and the meaning of contemporary Scottishness. Harrower's *Blackbird* is the story of an exploitative sexual relationship and is set in the present but explores the way events from the past return to haunt the present. Maxwell's verse ballad is set in 1452 and dramatises the conflicts between a young James II and the Earl of Douglas. In *The Last Witch* Munro provides a fictional exploration of the real-life story of Janet Horne, the last woman in Britain to be burnt as a witch, set in the Highland town of Dornoch in 1727. Beaton's political satire *Caledonia* premièred at the 2010 Edinburgh International Festival in a co-production between the EIF and the NTS. The play is an exploration of Scotland's futile attempt at establishing a colony in Darien, Panama, which saw ships set sail from Leith in 1698. The mission ended in failure with the loss of over 2,000 lives, bankrupted Scotland and led to the 1707 Act of Union.

Burke's *Black Watch* has been especially important in bringing the past and politics back to the Scottish stage and positioning them centre stage. *Black Watch* opened at the Drill Hall, Forest Hill, Edinburgh in August 2006 and quickly became the must-see production of that summer, going on to win numerous awards, including four Oliviers and a New York Drama Critics' Circle Award for Best Foreign Play, and to tour extensively at home and abroad. As well as featuring narration, song, movement, stand-up comedy, film and politics, it additionally bears traces of its own historical moment: sections of the play are based on interviews with members of the famous Scottish regiment in 2004, a time when it was still fighting in Iraq and was also being forcibly integrated into the Royal Highland Regiment. The soldiers' stories are collected, ordered and placed within a broader historical narrative, 'The Golden Thread' – the regiment's grand meta-narrative of their own 300-year history.

Given 'the scale of its historical sweep and its innovative staging', *Black Watch* invites comparison with McGrath and 7:84 (Scotland)'s *The Cheviot*.[10] But history in the latter play is mobilised to very different ends. As Trish Reid has noted, 'McGrath sought to challenge establishment versions of history and replace them with a people's history that would reveal the mechanisms through which workers had been oppressed, in order that these mechanisms might be challenged'.[11] Within *Black Watch*, by contrast, Burke constructs 'a narrative of working-class male solidarity achieved through regional and generational commitment to military service within the context of the British Empire'.[12] Worryingly, the extent to which Scotland's Highland regiments were implicated in the imperial project is essentially glossed over within the play.

As in the 1970s and 80s, then, the 2000s have to date seen a clear tendency in Scottish playwriting to return to the past for political reasons. But what has arguably emerged in this newer boom of history plays is a closer focus on national identity as debates over Scotland's constitutional relationship with the UK have been brought more sharply into focus. Scotland's most celebrated contemporary playwright, David Greig, does just this in his recent history play, *Dunsinane*, which, as with Munro's new trilogy, is set in medieval Scotland.[13] Commissioned by the RSC in 2010 and revived the following year in a co-production with NTS, this revisionist sequel to *Macbeth* explores the question of what happens next – what happens after Macbeth has been killed and Malcolm takes the throne? More than this, Greig revisits the Macbeth story through a Scottish lens, inviting the audience to read the events that happened at Dunsinane against the grain of the traditional 'history' of Macbeth (and Scotland) that has come down to us since Shakespeare's time. The Scottish playwright can be seen to open up a space in which to construct an alternative and revised history of Macbeth. More than this, Greig lays claim to the Macbeth story in the name of Scotland's own cultural difference from England: interrogating the nature of empire control and the rebuilding of a kingdom, *Dunsinane* can ultimately be seen to call for a renegotiation of the current relationship between Scotland and England.

It is far from surprising that as Scotland faces its historic referendum, playwrights in increasing numbers are turning to the past, and especially to stories of the pre-Union past, in an attempt to think through and explore urgent questions about the nation – what it should be, what it should become. This concern with history shown by contemporary Scottish playwrights, as with those who experimented with the history play in the 1590s and more recently in the 1970s and 80s, is absolutely rooted in their concern with the present and developing state of their nation – as they tap into and examine the past, their true interest lies in the Scotland of now.

As Peter Ustinov's President of 'the Smallest Country in Europe' in *Romanoff and Juliet* (1956) says, 'the great virtue of history is that it is adaptable'.[14] By premiering so close to the independence referendum, Rona Munro's adaptation of historical narratives in *The James Plays* undoubtedly served to demand space in which to consider and debate the various options open to the people of Scotland regarding the governance of their nation.

Endnotes

1 National Theatre of Scotland 2014 Programme, p. 4. http://www.national theatrescotland.com.

2 *The James Plays* trilogy is NTS's fifth co-production with the EIF – the previous productions are *Realism* (2006), *The Bacchae* (2007), *365* (2008) and *Caledonia* (2010) – and its first co-production between NTS and the National Theatre of Great Britain.

3 Dominique Goy-Blanquet, 'Elizabethan Historiography and Shakespeare's Sources', *The Cambridge Companion to Shakespeare's History Plays*, ed. Michael Hattaway, Cambridge University Press, 2002, p. 69.

4 One of the seminal texts of modern Scottish history, T.C. Smout's *A History of the Scottish People* was published in 1969.

5 Ian Brown, 'Plugged into History: the Sense of the Past in Scottish Theatre', *Scottish Theatre Since the Seventies*, ed. Randall Stevenson and Gavin Wallace. Edinburgh University Press, 1996, pp. 85-86.

6 Brown, 'Plugged into History'.

7 Brown, 'Plugged into History', p. 88.

8   David Archibald, 'History in Contemporary Scottish Theatre', *The Edinburgh Companion to Scottish Drama*, ed. Ian Brown, Edinburgh University Press, 2011, p. 86.

9   Archibald, 'History in Contemporary Scottish Theatre', p. 89.

10 Archibald, 'History in Contemporary Scottish Theatre', p. 93.

11 Trish Reid, *Theatre & Scotland*, Palgrave Macmillan, 2013, p. 17.

12 Reid, p. 17.

13 David Greig's other history plays include *The Cosmonaut's Last Message to the Woman He Once Loved in the Former Soviet Union* (1999), set in the closing days of the former Soviet Union, and *Victoria* (2000), a one-act play set in the Highlands in 1936, 1976 and 1996, in which he reflects on the changing nature of politics, both local and global.

14 Peter Ustinov, *Romanoff and Juliet*, in *Five Plays*, Heinemann, 1965, p. 55.

Rachael Boast

Poems from *Dark Saying*

Author's Note: The following poems arose from the preoccupation with a detail concerning Arthur Rimbaud, who, in about 1872, had collected under the proposed title, 'Études néantes' ('Void studies'), a short series of poems which in the spirit of musical études went beyond the temptation to convey any direct message. The book never materialised.

Afterlife

Late nights like unopened letters
the fold coming unstuck

from this one in the moist air
the message made prescient

by the way in which a wave
lifting from the surface of itself

could be lifted further
enough to reach into it and grasp

from under its erratic stars
the unwritten hour before dawn

A Second Time

Time stops where the vision
left off and the miracles began

the freak fall of snow
storm that opened the inner door

then the front and back until
the walls turned deep red

home was not where home was
the hallway an impossible wind tunnel

for the swarm you left behind
the door by chance still open

Return of the Song

Notes on the tongue
with the right measure

of air at play between
the image of song

and of wine
in double staves

heard in our land
a high contralto

becoming the key
to the door of the wind

Seeing Double

Waning in a far sign again I return to her
carrying the secret of the night

the colour of a dawn sun above a horizon
of tree tops in a pointed sky strung

with the starlight of slow moving time
clarified in the mirror where she rises

slipping from one bright hour to another
seeing double not from the corner of my eye

but from the middle looking again
as she couples her fortune of silver

Sunday

The smell of sunlight on river water
in shocks and tints ruins the calm mirror

of sleep and the disciplines of the dark.
The pushy oars of rowers dissemble and mark

the surface leaving a trail of peacock eyes
in their wake while half-asleep in the ultraviolet

I almost believe in the sky's huge blue terrace
trembling. I've seen you shield yourself from this

fabulous Chaos that the day springs on us,
dreaming yourself awake in fits and starts.

Testament

In my sleep the figure in a dream
chiselling at a rock face

in the Lomond Hills
reveals through the granite's

dark weather some golden lettering
which causes sweating.

As ever, it is night without end
in a place that doesn't begin

yet he keeps rising to his task
caught up in the echo of his work.

Dream of the Poem

This side of the night you're a blues singer
who sees everything that's going on

in the bar and with soft eyes notices
a stranger in the corner with his hands folded

over his hat. The name of the bar, Heaven,
and in the basement of Heaven, wine ageing

in oak barrels in the dark of the moon.
The stranger, who says he is asleep, dreams

of unpicked grapes growing full on the vine
that has wound itself around you.

Atrocious fanfare

Stopping for lunch of meat and wine
in the Maison Bleue on the off chance

you weren't there so the waitress took
your glass and by the second one

I was ascending to heaven
via the usual hellish path

to the sound of falling cutlery
while the undreamed-of work

transforms into a golden hurrah
and with this I refill your missing glass.

You tried the door

The first drops of rain, a pulse in the leaves,
enough to make aspirin by rubbing

my fingers where my fingers shouldn't be.
Something here remains of love

in the slow hours of imagined time
recovering in the afterlife almost as good

as what came before I searched on both sides
trying to relocate myself where you are

a downpour and a flash of light under
the willow, under the rose, under the night.

Château néant

Door after door but with the same key
of cold iron unlocking them all

one to another leading on
to the room in the middle of nowhere

where you go to work the forge
of the dream of disrepair lit by rapid

fragments of light. Stones sweat gold
silver and copper. A swarm of bees

appears from hammered metal
leaving an aftertaste of black honey.

Tracey Emerson

Seaview

Grace sees him for the first time on a Sunday afternoon at the Seaview Residential Care Home. He is wrestling a magazine from a shrivelled, silver-haired woman in the TV lounge.

'Let go, Mum,' he says. 'Please.' He is tall, and his full head of black hair contains only a few streaks of grey. Fit and muscular in his jeans and navy blue sweatshirt, he radiates vitality amongst all the weakness and demise. Grace hovers in the lounge doorway, forgetting she was on her way to the garden for some fresh air and a break from her own mother.

'It's mine.' A man with a long, white beard points at the torn magazine from the prison of his beige armchair. Lisa, one of the care assistants, pats him on the shoulder.

'She doesn't know what she's doing, love. She doesn't mean it.'

The mother lets go of her shredded prize and strikes her son's face.

'Get off me you little cunt,' she screams. Then she stops, as if her batteries have run out and falls to her knees. She glances around the room and seems shocked to find herself there. The sobbing starts. Frustrated, childlike sobbing.

'It's okay. I've got you.' Her son reaches down and scoops her up. Grace steps aside as he carries his mother out of the room, accompanied by several longing sighs. A warped version of the famous scene from *An Officer and a Gentleman*.

She returns to her mother's room.

'I'm back,' she says.

The boxy room is a pharaoh's tomb, a gap stop between worlds crammed with treasured possessions – family photographs, a stack of Daniel O'Donnell CDs and a collection of crystal swans. An antique carriage clock provides a loud, second by second reminder of lost time from the bedside table.

Her mother lies motionless in a narrow single bed. Eyes closed, mouth open, each breath accompanied by a frothy, gurgling noise, as if she is drowning. The chest infection she developed three days ago might still result in an admission to hospital but so far, so good. Grace has slept on a fold down bed beside her mother for the past two nights. She is tired and fragile and longing to get back to London. She is dressed in the same jeans and black polo neck jumper she arrived in on Friday. Her armpits are sticky and odorous. Her dark, curly hair is greasy and tied back in a ponytail. All she wants is a hot bath and a large glass of red wine.

She opens the window just wide enough to steal a few gulps of cool, October air. The oak tree at the centre of the garden is on the turn, leaves rusting. Soon it will be stripped bare.

Her mother emits a low, tortured moan. Grace shuts the window.

'I'm here.'

She sits beside the bed. Her mother's right hand, the only part of her stroke-weary body still functioning, scratches a path across the bedcover. Grace lifts the cold, dry fingers to her lips and kisses them.

'I'm here.'

She misses her father, ten years dead. She misses the siblings she has never had. She feels older than her forty-five years and she feels alone.

Not quite alone.

Another version of her lurks in the room, the one her mother longed for. Grace the Wed and Bred. For an instant, Grace shares this longing. A child would provide a joyous, noisy distraction for both of them.

Instead here they are. Grace and her mother with only the ticking clock for company.

Two women at the end of their line.

Later, desperate for respite, she heads to the visitors' kitchen to make herself a drink.

There he is. Slumped at the yellow Formica table, head in hands. He looks up when she enters and they introduce themselves. Grace. Carl.

'Yes,' he replies, when she asks if he is from Folkestone, 'lived here all my life.' He tells her he is a chartered surveyor, and she tells him she teaches English to foreign businessmen.

She glances at his wedding finger and sees the thick gold band there.

She makes him a coffee – black, two sugars – and a peppermint tea for herself. She joins him at the table and they talk about their hometown. The way things were before the Tunnel, the schools they'd attended. Anything to avoid their mothers.

'Seaview Residential Care Home,' she says, aware she is rambling. 'Have you noticed how everything in Folkestone is called Seaview? Even when there isn't one.'

Carl smiles. 'I like your voice.'

'Oh.' Heat rushes up her neck. 'Really?'

'Yes.'

Soon Carl will be calling her at least twice a week to listen to her voice. The calls will come without warning. She might be stacking the dishwasher, clipping her toenails, adding strips of chicken to a smouldering wok.

'Tell me a story,' he'll say.

She will picture him with his zip undone, ready to go. In his bathroom maybe, or on his marital bed, tissues at hand to remove the evidence.

She will tell him a story. The two of them meeting as strangers in a park on a hot day. Her in a floaty dress without underwear. Sitting on his lap under the shade of a leafy tree. His fingers inside her. His gasps and groans will echo down the phone as he touches himself, and she will touch herself too.

At first she will marvel at her inventiveness, at the variety of settings and characters and positions that pour out of her, but later, especially towards the end, she will want to talk about the Tube strike that made her late for work, or the weather, or the fact that her aging boiler has broken down again. She will want to warn him that the future is coming but will listen to him coming instead.

She knows none of this as she sips her peppermint tea and Carl gulps back his coffee. The story she is sharing with him now – and she can't believe she is sharing it with a stranger – is the one about losing her virginity to Jamie Inglis at the Seaview Bed and Breakfast when she was sixteen.

'See what I mean?' she says. 'Always Seaview.'

Jamie, her first love, with his frayed grey cardigan, his monkey boots and his Morrissey quiff.

'We signed the guest book as The Smiths,' she says.

She and Carl will visit hotels together, not guest houses. She will make the bookings and secure them with her credit card, and Carl will pay for the rooms in cash. In these discrete hotels he will pretend that his real life does not exist. She will collude with him, despite knowing that she shouldn't.

Carl drops his head into his hands again and takes long, deep breaths. When he surfaces, his eyes are glazed. 'Good job euthanasia isn't legal,' he says. 'It'd be bloody tempting.'

Her laughter is high and false. His is harsh and desperate.

'I know,' she says. Her throat is hot and tight, a sign she might cry if she's not careful. 'The whole parent-child reversal thing is such a lame deal. I mean they chose to have us but we didn't choose them. At least when we were crapping ourselves we were cute.'

Their hands meet on the cold Formica. Fingers interlock. His thumb finds the centre of her palm and treats her flesh to a gentle massage. His touch lures her tears into the open.

The touch of his tongue will do this one afternoon in one of those hotel rooms. The tenderness of him between her thighs, the time he will take over her. At one point he will look up.

'This is only for you,' he'll say. 'I don't do this for anyone but you.'

As if he is giving her diamonds.

In the visitors' kitchen, Grace stands up.

'Come on,' she says.

She leads Carl out into the corridor. They dodge a hunchbacked man pushing a zimmer frame and a care assistant with a tea-trolley. Carl's hand is on her back as they hurry down two flights of stairs to the basement.

She pushes open the door to the laundry room. Warm, cottony air envelops them as soon as they step inside. Machines whir and rattle mid-cycle. The door of one of the tumble dryers is open, a tussle of pale blue sheets half-delivered into the waiting basket.

Carl locks the door behind them.

It happens fast. Frantic, painful kissing. His hands fumble with her belt as she unbuttons and unzips him.

'I'm married,' he says.

'I know.'

'Got three kids.'

'Don't need to know.'

Her last meeting with Carl will be in a hotel room panelled with dark wood. The bed will be covered with a purple satin bedspread and far too many pillows. They will find a use for the writing desk, the wall and the floor before finally collapsing onto the bed, gleaming with sweat.

The black, lacy bra and knickers he bought for her to wear will be strewn across the purple carpet. As she stares at them, Grace will realise she has just enacted one of Carl's fantasies and that she could be anybody. This will make her angry, and this anger will escalate when Carl takes a bottle of Sainsbury's own brand champagne from the mini-bar.

'Brought your own?' she'll say. 'Aren't I worth mini-bar prices?'

By this time her mother will have been dead three weeks, and Grace will have learned that mothers are like lift cables. Out of sight and unappreciated, keeping life's machinery moving smoothly up and down. Until they die and then comes the plummet. In the wood-panelled room she will still be in freefall. Emotions no longer under her control.

Carl will sigh. As he pours her a drink she will notice the Debenhams carrier bag underneath the writing desk.

'What's that?' she'll say.

'Something for my eldest. She's thirteen next week.'

The girl's intrusion into the room will make Grace shiver and reach for the satin bedspread.

'You can talk about your kids whenever you want,' she'll say. 'I don't mind.' She will sound as uncertain as she feels.

'I know.' Carl will stare at the floor as he says this. She will know then that the gift is an omen and that Carl can no longer keep his two worlds separate. Soon he will sacrifice this temporary pleasure for his lasting happiness.

'I want to make love,' she'll say.

'We just did.'

'That wasn't making love.'

'Grace.'

'Please.'

He will soon be inside her again, but his gentleness will only convince her that she is condemned.

'Look at me,' he'll say.

She will try but too much will occur to her at once. That she has never had sex in order to create a child and that the time to do so has almost certainly passed. That Carl is at her core, opening her up, and she may never be able to close herself again.

That for him she will be nothing but a surface wound, one his busy life will soon seal over.

'Grace.' His final whisper in her ear.

When he ejaculates there will be a fizzing deep within her, tiny celebratory fireworks, her body still fooled, even though she knows the influx of semen is pointless.

After he withdraws, Carl will go to the bathroom, closing the door behind him. She will lie there, his redundant sperm seeping down her leg. Before he returns and the conversation about their end begins, she will slip a finger into herself and dab the sticky mixture they've created onto her tongue.

Kissing in the laundry room of the Seaview Residential Care Home. Carl pushes her backwards towards the sink unit until the hard edge of the draining board digs into her lower back.

'Turn around,' he says.

The ridged metal is cool against her left cheek and smells of bleachy lemons.

'I'm not on the pill,' she says. 'You'll have to –'

'Had a vasectomy,' he says as he pushes into her.

'Good.'

She shuts her eyes, focuses on the rhythm of him. She urges him on, urges him to fuck everything out of her. Everything everything everything, until nothing but peace remains.

Paul Batchelor

Standing Male Nude

Squat, blunt, built for work –
the Northumbrian physique:
broad chest, short legs, long back –
though the relic of that six pack
is seen only by believers
these days, by true lovers:
the pure of heart, the elect.
The cock, lately erect,
looks rueful, bloodless, shrunk
after its wash in the sink;
and there's something girlish – is
it the long eyelashes
or the soft, small hands or
something in the demeanour?

He's not a worker, this one.
He's a learned person.
On those thin ankles he's
top-heavy as a horse,
well watered and well fed
with all he can afford –
this room with its mini-bar,
Toblerone and small beer.

The hour of the wolf,
and he's subjecting himself
to a quick once-over:
furred tongue, howling hangover –
but no visible scars,
no motive, no obvious clues…

Early-bird, self-admirer
reporting to the mirror,
in the hum of the fluorescent
he lingers, fascinated
by an almost-handsome face –
thirty-something, but he'd pass
for thirty-something-else…
Closer scrutiny reveals
(sketched-in, an afterthought)
the outline of a shirt,
perhaps, shook out on the bed,
and what could that be but
the yet-to-be-toppled skittle
of a whisky bottle?

The Seven Joys of Failure

The first joy of failure
is relief at the success avoided:
more properly, the consequences of success;
and the prospect of a quietude,
absence of ambition
passing for humility.

The second joy
is pecuniary, for when vision is reduced
to the things of the world
it will most often find itself accompanied
by the sorts of behaviours
that go with, lead to, or derive from, money.

The third joy
is private and hardly to be spoken of;
but joy nonetheless, however gruesome,
at having our self-loathing proven true,
the certainty so many tender doubts defended
rudely confirmed.

The fourth joy
is public: at the warmth of fellow-feeling,
the heartiness of the embrace,
smiling enquiries as to our future plans
if any, unstinting camaraderie,
the glad-hand welcome of the world.

The fifth joy
is the sweetest joy: the care of the clear-eyed
who supported us without belief,
and built a store for the inevitable day
we thought would never come:
day of their triumph.

The sixth joy
is dangerous: the temptation to believe
that something may yet come of this;
that we have fallen into wakefulness
merely to enact the dream;
that the final crash was but a station.

The seventh joy
is satisfaction: claiming the comfortable chair
from which we see life in a true perspective,
and things as we suppose they are
align with every circumstance:
never to rise, never to want again.

Vidyan Ravinthiran

Stair Steps

Last summer my girlfriend's brother got married in Romania. The bride's family, Orthodox Christian – other faiths, especially Greek Catholicism, were stamped on, if not out, by the Communists – live in Cluj-Napoca: a city whose chaotic wiring against the sky could be compared either to a spider's web or the radial cracks in a smashed windscreen. An even grey warmth as one strolls the cobbles and big courtyards; a sense of the countryside encroaching into the city rather than the other way round. The peach-coloured churches are ornate not finicky: dusk-enhanced, and enhancing. In the run-up to the wedding we dined with the parents. Romanians are tremendous hosts – gestural, super-attentive, their social rituals are unhampered by smaller proprieties. Much wine and clear plum liqueur was consumed and Tony, Ana's father (his wife, Olimpia, speaks little English, and Romanian men are very much the heads of their families, or think they are) remarked of the humiliations of life under Communism that we couldn't possibly understand. Except he didn't say *couldn't*, or *possibly* – that's how an English person (my parents, never) would talk. He was angry and not at us; then grinned as we watched the bride and groom practice their waltz around the living room.

A day or two before the ceremony we were driven to a hilltop monastery – ordered blooms, a head-clearing coolness, pointed wooden steeples like witches' hats; then to The Memorial of the Victims of Communism and of the Resistance at Sziget. This 150-mile drive took us right up to the Ukrainian border. We saw the horse-drawn carts familiar to English viewers from hysterical news reports on immigration; handmade hay-bales of different shapes and even colours; small platforms affixed to telephone poles for storks to build their nests on. Tony pointed out with delight the glimmer of pots and pans on a wooden stoop – they announce to the community a daughter of marriageable age.

It was late when we reached the Sziget Museum and only Tony's cajoling got us in. By this point his determination was quietly obvious – this was something we had to see. The building used to be a prison. You move from room to room learning of one atrocity after another. On the ground floor, one finds the cell where Iuliu Maniu, a former Prime Minister of Romania and supporter of the Allies during the war years, was incarcerated following a show trial and died in 1953; another room discusses the operations of the Securitate, or Communist Secret Police, between 1948 and the revolution of 1989 which saw off Ceaușescu. Both the paper guide and the legends on the walls of the prison museum can be hard for an English-speaker to follow, especially when hurried – yet a particular sentence stuck with me, which I find reproduced on the website. It is mysterious and disturbing and follows a paragraph of angered detail about the Securitate's 'methodical programme of mass indoctrination and manipulation', its strategies of public humiliation and stirring up of 'conflicts between the different segments' of the populace; the repression of even 'the smallest gesture of independence by intellectuals'. We are then told – the contortions interest – that 'despite these draconian measures, the end of the Ceaușescu regime could not be avoided, but the traces of this violation of national consciousness persist even today in the mentality of many members of the public.'

We never made it to room 51, which features the verse of political prisoners and suggests that for Romanians living under Communism, poetry was a revolutionary force; a mainstay of national identity as well as an underground river of dissident thought. One thinks of the Czech poet Miroslav Holub, and the many Poles – Milosz, Różewicz, Herbert, Syzmborska – who belong now to the canon of twentieth-century verse. They are, in translation, our classics, authors of global authority. The same cannot yet be said for Ana Blandiana, who helped found the memorial at Sziget. She is certainly a figure of tremendous prestige in Romania, having written countless books of verse and also prose, many of which have been at one time or other banned. Individually persecuted (Ana Blandiana is a pseudonym chosen by a poet whose father was a political prisoner; it didn't protect her for long) she was a well-known opponent of the Romanian Communist Party, and in 2009 received the Legion of Honour. Yet before the publication by Bloodaxe of *My Native Land A4* (the meaning is that the blank page is her only true homeland; that, as we must repeat of all good poets cursed and blessed with political subject-matter, Blandiana is not merely or programmatically political) English readers had to make do with a slender Selected, *The Hour of Sand*. This book, translated by Peter Jay and Anca Cristofovici, is published by Anvil Press; the homepage says it will 'be available again soon'. I deeply hope this is the case, since it is as fine a book as the Bloodaxe, and also expresses uniquely the complications of its historical moment.

Take for instance 'You Never See the Butterflies', a wryly excited poem which could be read in very different ways. How the title is at one with the originating perception is usual for Blandiana. Her poems are impulsive, they take off from an initial confusion or conceit and resemble the bright unanswerable query of a child:

> You never see
> The butterflies, how they look at each other above us?
> Nor the signs that the wind
> Makes to the grass as we walk by?
> If I suddenly turn,
> The branches are struck dumb
> And wait for us to move on.
> Haven't you noticed the birds are setting
> Haven't you noticed the leaves are going out?
> Haven't you noticed the whispers
> Growing on our backs,
> Like moss on the side of tree-trunks facing north?

The first line is brilliantly frustrated; the second has bugger all to do with butterflies. It has an impatience – *why don't you understand?* – the poem goes on to complicate. I'm reminded of that sentence at Sziget about a mutilation of the national consciousness – which might yet redeem itself. A bad, clamped feeling not without lyrical content, a little movement upwards out of the dirt. Blandiana uses and re-uses a set of natural props, but deceptively. Birds, unlike the sun, don't set, and leaves, unlike fires, don't go out, so even before the outright metaphor of the whispers growing on people as moss does on tree-trunks, we arrive in a strange world. Nothing works quite right here;

there are rules which run contrary to natural laws. As she writes elsewhere, the 'sunset is rancid / And the sunrise faked'.

So, reading *The Book of Sand* from cover to cover, I was rather confused by Jay and Cristofovici's apolitical, rather hedged introduction, which describes this poem as 'visionary' and 'worthy of Samuel Palmer', authored by a 'convinced Romantic who feels that fundamental values are under direct threat'; whose 'strong religious or spiritual impulse' relates primarily to 'the animistic world of Romanian folk poetry and fairy tale'. True, Blandiana is a Romantic, a responsibly dilapidated visionary: she returns over and over again to the interaction between the self and a natural world she still believes enchanted. The butterflies, the wind, the branches – the world responds to us, it isn't dead matter. Yet there's surely another reading. This is a poem about being spied on. *Et in Arcadia ego:* like death itself, the secret police are present in the landscape – they are the hidden second meaning we must attend to. Butterflies, wind, branches: the poet defends herself against surveillance by developing a code of her own. And even the title isn't really a non-title, drawn from the first line and a half – it's ominous. The butterflies, you never see them coming.

The distance between this reading and the translators' reveals the curious bind, the closet of bad faith, one finds oneself in with poets like Blandiana. We seek from the verse of Eastern Europe a uniquely tested authenticity; deliverance from the accusation that poetry is a self-regarding middle-class hobby. In their world, poets remain arbiters of culture and speak on behalf of the dispossessed. Historical suffering is present in these poems as a kind of chiaroscuro; a halo of shadow, a guarantee of weight, significance; an explicit holiness or an oblique thrill. The editorial structure of *The Book of Sand* resonates for this reason. For its afterword doesn't actually come at the end of the book, but precedes a handful of explicitly political poems ('Everything', or 'Totul', parodies one of Ceauşescu's vocal tics; 'I believe' describes Romanians as a 'vegetal people'). Unlike the introduction, it labels the book

a product of the age of the dictatorship and the long arm of Ceauşescu's repression and censorship. The December uprising took place between the printing of the first edition's cover and of its text. For fear of making Ana Blandiana's life in Bucharest more difficult than it had been, our

Introduction could only hint at the nature of the 'direct threat' to her country's fabric and values, or at the 'circumstances beyond her control' which caused her third banning in autumn 1988. But we decided not to change it, since it focuses on values rather than on circumstances, which are likely to be unsettled for some time.

The final sentence puzzles somewhat, though of course the focus on values rather than circumstances continues Blandiana's project, insisting that the individual isn't simply a product of history, that beliefs and feelings do matter and do have a meaning which survives authoritarian distortion. These poems, Jay and Cristofovici suggest, have a meaning which isn't political; and perhaps this is the delayed, the secret, the true meaning. The structure of *The Book of Sand*, with its tricksy introduction and clarifying afterword, may have been necessitous. Yet it also lets the verse breathe, making the real and difficult claim that the spiritual content of Blandiana's work isn't subsidiary, but as uncomfortably and valuably there as the politics we're all too apt to consider the final guarantor of poetic significance.

That said, there are poems here which it would be unjust, reductive, to treat as unmoored thought experiments inconsiderate of Romanian history. 'Perhaps Someone is Dreaming Me', for one, is not simply a Borgesian conceit, but a description of what it is like to live under a regime which ideologically mutilates history, trashing old-style understandings of oneself and others:

> That's why my gestures
> Are so soft
> And unfinished,
> With their aim forgotten
> Half-way,
> Grotesquely,
> That's why my outlines get blurred
> Second by second
> And my deeds melt…

What terrifies and enthrals is the poem's 'that's why'. The speaker tries to make sense of her situation, also to state clearly to the reader (really I want to say listener; these poems are vividly, urgently spoken) what exactly the problem is. Which of course sends us back to the horrifying political facts. Many of Blandiana's poems try on a particular metaphor – for understanding life; each is eventually revealed as good enough only for the moment, a stance of momentary confidence. There is an element of play, but these lyrics are really prayers, which exist to salve the world-weary and be activated by the desperate. Each perishable framework seeks to briefly alleviate, or at least clarify, a vast, implicitly understood suffering which touches on what used to be called the human condition, but also maintains a definitively Romanian content. And this two-way pull begs the question: should we read her to try and understand her country better, or is there something here which, without being morally complacent, is genuinely for us too? The prison paragraphs of Sziget were hard to follow: these poems let me in.

Contrary to modern assumptions, the individual I describe as the 'speaker' of these poems really must be identified with Blandiana herself, a cultural spokesperson of gendered heroism: an oracle, a bastion of impassioned purity, a voice whose vulnerability rhymes with and expresses that of millions. In the afterword to *My Native Land A4*, she writes:

> Maybe I should be offended by this total dependence on forces that I cannot even minimally influence, but I feel happy and as proud as a lady in waiting that the king has chosen to bear his child. This is an odd combination of humility and pride that can only result in a special form of liberation. I was convinced until recently that I write because someone inside of me dictates, word for word, something that I have to hurriedly write down, and that I only have to create the necessary conditions for this inner voice to speak, and not stop speaking.

It's almost reminiscent of Elizabeth I – how Blandiana accepts a particular understanding of herself as a passive woman which she then seriously empowers. ('I have never been able to say "we poets" without embarrassment', she remarks, 'just as I have never been able to say "we women" without blushing.') Those 'forces' she skulks before and cannot influence aren't governmental or military. She speaks of 'moments of grace', of transgressive inspiration; the imaginative energies a poet depends on and couldn't hope to administer. Yet it does *sound* like she's talking about state control: really, this rhetoric is how Blandiana turns necessity into freedom. If the poet is put upon, harassed, dominated – a Romanian citizen – she can at least describe the forces which control her however she wishes. She can choose (like a voter in a genuinely democratic system) what they are. The laws which ultimately compel, which terrify and liberate, are, she tells us (makes us feel, from poem to poem) not those of rotten tyrants but truths elemental; religious; creative. The restless urgencies of the spirit.

'The Owner of the Mill', published in the new collection, describes a figure who is to God what Blandiana's infamous satirical tomcat – in a banned children's poem – was to Ceauşescu. That is: as precise a portrait as may be allowed, as will outrun the red pencil of the censor. Which in this case means the internalised, historically dejected voice of secular realism:

> What is it made of,
> That dust that he leaves over things,
> So fine (it's almost invisible)
> It only duplicates their contours with a halo of shadow?
> Where is the mill that grinds down everything that disappears
> And produces this sawdust of non-being?
> Like a powder that sticks to your fingers
> When you want to caress something out of the past.
> Or maybe he's the one who's been ground up,
> So that no one will notice when he disappears
> And no one will remember
> The difference between
> The finite cold
> And burning eternity.
> But in that case, who is the owner of that mill where
> Death is nothing but a pale manipulation?

Earlier I applied a phrase from this poem – 'halo of shadow' – to Blandiana's political verse. Here that extra dimension of significance is religious. Yet there is, again, overlap – we don't know who or what the poet's thinking of. A being removed from power, who still conditions the world; people don't remember, their responses are inadequate. Questions are asked, as in 'You Never See the Butterflies', but they're dominated by the impossible desire to take something airy and invisible and admire its texture between one's fingers.

The sounds of the poem are delicious – each *l* and *t*, how *duplicates* links up with *halo* and is eventually transformed into *manipulation* (not, here, that of the Securitate); an awkward compliment to pay translated verse, because one doesn't know quite who to pat on the head, or if the felicities are accidental, even. But I think the new translators, Paul Scott Derrick and Viorica Patea, must be praised. It's absolutely the right thing to have 'where' come trippingly off the penultimate line instead of making the last a shade too solid, portentous. And the rhythm of the first four lines in particular is brilliantly fluid – even the double 'that' sandwiching 'dust' seems to work (you come down harder on the first than the second), although the deixis does appear many times in the book, and could be trimmed. But perhaps the optional 'that' expresses something of Romanian diction: I don't know. (There's a similar effect in 'Stele', which describes of the symbol above a child's gravestone 'the fingers spread out / As though to ward off something, / That something that cannot be detained by empty hands'.) Certainly the effect of precision is essential to Blandiana – the making-sense-of-things, the cautious open-endedness.

'Caress', which the translators link up acoustically with 'past', is an equally important word in 'On Tiptoe':

> I have tiptoed
> Up to the line,
> I only wanted to touch it
>   With the tip of my naked foot,
> Like in summer, when I caress the line
>   Between the land and the sea.
> But the boundary drew back
> As though it wanted to protect itself from me –
> I keep going forward
> Over this sand moistened by death,
> Alive and proud
> That I can push that frontier back
> Or, perhaps, just step over it
> Unawares.

About a self-aware poem there are obvious remarks to be made about the poetic 'foot' and 'line', and Blandiana's afterword does describe 'the work of art itself' as 'that tenuous and imprecise boundary between existence and non-existence'. This modest poem's one great line – I'm speaking of the 'sand moistened by death' – reveals that talent crucial to the philosophical poet, of fusing the sensuous detail with a description of reality. Touch matters to Blandiana. The present moment obtrudes its sensuousness, as if asking: *why fly off into the past, its questions of the spirit? Isn't this, aren't I, enough?* And there's a beautiful elegy in this book for the poet's mother. But still she resists merely individual subject-matter, and with it idiosyncrasy of style: 'related more with the desire to cause sensation than to be, the pursuit of originality seems to me frivolous'. What isn't frivolous is what connects one spirit to another, as the poet, touching on the old and permanent, the ley-lines of being, speaks to and for all. Everyone who has been to the sea has played with the tide, with tingling feet –we know what this is like. *Caress,* and the death-moistened sand, represent the poet's more specialised contribution, yet Blandiana would have us recognise these details just as intimately.

Blandiana's longing for an organic community redemptive of modern displacement is both nostalgic and utopian, and it's relevant here that Romania went industrial only in the middle of the twentieth century – its economic and technological development has been, is, bitty, deflected, partial. So 'Agglomeration' yearns for a vanished world of enchanted ritual, in which 'every square inch of ground was inhabited / By endless hierarchies of invisible beings'. Yet this desire is ironised – 'How marvellous to walk around among them / And not to bother anyone' – perhaps because the poem speaks out of complicated feelings here about the more actual and dangerously recent past:

> What an exciting life! What tumultuous emotions,
> When even the smallest event was shepherded by a god
> That had to be prayed to, begged and adored –
> A god that extorted sacrifices – i.e., metaphysical bribes –
> In order to carry out his appointed duties.

'Agglomeration' records the caprice of deities in terms recalling a poisoned bureaucracy. Blandiana's nostalgia is self-critical – it can't help but turn into caustic allegory. It is as if, wishing for a world of unpredictable and irrational magic, charged with constant meaning, it hits her suddenly she's talking about life in the Socialist Republic.

The risk for a political poet whose has accomplished her goal in the negative sense – the destruction of Communism – but not the positive (Blandiana is clearly unthrilled by the corruption and ahistorical consumerism of present-day Romania) is that of subsiding into either sophisticated resignation or reactionary bitterness. 'On Roller Skates' approaches a rant about the youth with 'earphones droning in their ears / and their eyes glued to monitors'; 'Season's End' describes a universe filled with 'dust forgotten in the corners / And empty warehouses / Where meaningless poems are declaimed.' Yet Blandiana is ultimately a deeply generous poet – when too weary for optimism, she is nonetheless intelligently earnest. Lines strongly reminiscent of *The Waste Land* ask where history went wrong, but also suggest of civilisation itself a spiritual reality which outgoes hubris:

> Athens, Carthage, Rome,
> Byzantium, Constantinople, Istanbul,
> Waves of rubble,
> Stair steps
> To the doorway
> (That doesn't, in fact, exist)
> Of eternity.

'Stair Steps', the poem's called, not 'Waves of Rubble': Blandiana is mordant about, she doesn't outright reject, the impossible aspirations of perishable cultures. A grain of the unearthly is no bad thing; it's already positive, to claim this is where humans start out from, rather than self-interest, self-protection, a tyrannous expansionism. That the doorway between eternity and the earthly polis doesn't exist doesn't mean we shouldn't build the stair. A postmodern theology: one believes in God precisely because he doesn't exist.

On leaving the prison museum at Sziget we were led – hurriedly; it was well after closing-hours – through the courtyard of anguished sculptures and down into a darkened chamber with a water basin. A small fee buys a candle you insert into one of the small holes so its reflected flame joins the others. "You don't have to,' said our hosts kindly; afterwards, Olimpia bought us ice cream down the road. A marvellously understanding gesture. And since we can only begin to understand others using what's presently available, accessible, to us, I thought then – having not yet read Blandiana – of Michael Longley's 'All of These People':

> Who was it who suggested that the opposite of war
> Is not so much peace as civilisation? He knew
> Our assassinated Catholic greengrocer who died
> At Christmas in the arms of our Methodist minister,
> And our ice-cream man whose continuing requiem
> Is the twenty-one flavours children have by heart.
> Our cobbler mends shoes for everyone; our butcher
> Blends into his best sausages leeks, garlic, honey;
> Our cornershop sells everything from bread to kindling.
> Who can bring peace to people who are not civilised?
> All of these people, alive or dead, are civilised.

Ana Blandiana's *The Hour of Sand: Selected Poems 1969–1989* is published by Anvil Press, (£6.95) and *My Native Land A4* by Bloodaxe, (£9.95)

Nicola Nathan

Thumbelina's House of Magic

What were you waiting for? New fruit on frozen vines?
There was never that –
just a house of mirrors where the sun

set upside down in glass; the air was salt as quartz in rock,
the pathways steep and lost in fog.
She held your face through images which seemed to be two things at once:

girl and hag; man and beast.
She knew you as the hare that fled leaving a hint like breath in mist.
Step back to see the girl who combs her hair

beneath a chain of lights. She sits inside a painted skull –
her back's the socket of the nose, her hands are black held up
like shutters on the dead man's eyes;

the absence in her own dark stare suggests the earth is damp with rain:
you didn't see her levitate, her body float as dust in light;
you didn't watch her fall through glass, the trail of narratives and knives.

Portraits

His camera

Later, he would use the photograph as proof
that he'd stopped to make a fog above the Dart
and posed the children on a fallen log.

All else was down to me – the puddles and acorns,
moss grown on the inside of the rock, tree roots
lifting in the flood. I couldn't hear him

for the sound of his plans – the children
fixing coppers in the money tree;
the shutter stiff and locked against the day.

Her canvas

Now I catch what rests outside the lens:
the shadow of the bird that crossed your wrist;
the brushes in my hand, feathered like wings.

Look down... Look away... Look at me. This is your face –
this line is something like my flight between you
and the paint. The darkness set around you is my sky.

Thumbelina's Stutter

She stops just short of shadow. Even if
they threw a stone inside a well and listened
to the drop before the splash, it wouldn't help
them understand how darkness swallows sound.

Her ellipsis means... *this can't be said,* and when
in speech she cuts it close to something real,
the words arrive in French and slide around
their power. She's mist in mirrors: look away

and the sap's been drained from summer's beech;
ask about her breathlessness – she'll trace it
to the willow tree, a high wind lifting strips
of leaves, a sudden taste of ash and rain.

Cameron Conant

Husbandry

'I now pronounce you man and wife.'

'The fuck you do.'

The crowd gasps and turns.

Standing at the back is a man in his late forties wearing a John Deere cap and pit-stained t-shirt, Bahama shorts and a pair of flip-flops.

'You heard me, fucker. I object to this bullshit marriage.'

The preacher shuffles his feet. Adam's apple drops as he swallows. The bride's father stands up from the front row, points at the man in the back like he's aiming the barrel of a shotgun at a would-be burglar.

'Sheridan, I suggest you leave 'fore we have any trouble,' the red-faced father booms, voice ricocheting off 'a walls like stray bullets.

The bride is crying on the groom's shoulder, a skinny whip of a boy who just turned twenty-four. He's about to be her second husband, actually is by law, despite the fact that the couple hasn't even kissed yet. There's a mess of confetti in envelopes just waiting for the assembled to throw. There's nothing said for three seconds, but feels like thirty.

Sheridan's got meanness in his face, looks mad enough to spit, but so does the father, the retired Sheriff of Hartnett County. The old Sheriff's still pointing, then finally shouts, 'Move on, boy! Now!'

It's a stand-off. Some of the women have ducked beneath church pews on the off-chance firearms might be used. Both men carry. The pastor and newlyweds stand cemented up front, unable to move; a few people shake with silent sobs, including the groom's mama.

Silence makes even an experienced lawman like Sheriff uneasy, but he keeps his jaw clenched and that finger pointed like a weapon. Just when it seems as if Sheridan's going to go home and sleep off the booze, he unzips his pants and pulls his dick out. His wilted penis shoots piss down the center-aisle like the last dregs of water from a garden hose. That's when three men, two of them deacons, come out of nowhere and tackle Sheridan, getting urine-soaked and bruised in the process.

As Sheridan kicks and spins, one of the deacons punches him in the face and says it's for the bride's honor, which Sheridan's all but stolen, and has done for years and years. The John Deere cap is off and there are lines of blood in the carpet as they bind Sheridan's wrists with a necktie and the Sheriff puts a handgun to his back. They get him out on the front steps till the cop cars pull up with sirens.

The reception is almost silent. It's a Baptist wedding, which means no drink or dancing. Even in the best situations, Baptist weddings aren't a whole lot of fun, but even less so today, given that Sheridan did what he did. Those up for drinking will head to the bar afterwards.

When the couple cuts the cake, the twenty-four-year-old tries to spread frosting on the bride's face, like he's seen in movies and home videos. It's all in good fun, but her emotions are on edge, and it's enough to start the waterworks again. Soon, she's off to check her makeup, with a clutch of yellow-clad bridesmaids trailing her like baby chicks.

When she married Sheridan, she didn't have a real wedding to speak of, not one with fun, bright colors, and confetti, and a slideshow with baby pictures. She was six months pregnant and scared and ashamed. They kept the wedding small, with a stern talk from the preacher about the covenant they were entering into, and how God could redeem sin. Later, they had dinner at a hotel in their wedding clothes as people stared at Cassie's belly; sidelong glances that killed her appetite.

Sheridan first met her at the video store, which is where she worked when she was seventeen, fifteen years ago now. Sheridan was a mechanic then and almost two decades older than Cassie, an age gap that would've raised eyebrows with most. Cassie didn't even date boys, let alone men. Friends called Sheridan, 'Mutt', for reasons that were far from complicated. He was a bachelor who'd hump anything that moved. But he was always sweet to Cassie when he'd stop in to rent *Die Hard*.

'Why don't you just buy it?'

'I like talkin' to you.'

Never used any of his pick-up lines on her – 'let me take a look under your hood,' or 'need a tune up?' – way he did at Bar 64, Saturday nights, when he'd finish a few pitchers of beer with his buddies, then begin romancing the ladies as country music played loud.

One night, he convinced Cassie to go off with him after her shift at the video store. They started at a pond outside town, just talking about life, but ended up at Sheridan's one-acre piece of land in the sticks, playing cards on a fold-out table: Uno and Up the River-Down the River.

He got her drunk on PBR at the table, eventually turning the game into Strip Poker. Cassie lost big. She was shy as she stood before him, stripped naked, bronzed like a trophy. She had a crooked smile on her face, kept her eyes on her feet, counting freckles, as Sheridan sniffed around and made his approach. It was all over before she knew it.

Weeks later, the EPT turned pink, and she dropped out of school before graduation. Her daddy wanted to slap a statutory rape charge on Sheridan, but Sheridan had already managed to get Cassie interested in being his wife; plus he'd enrolled in community college, part-time, in order to earn his associate's at night. Not just that: he went and got clean-shaven, his hair trimmed, and even started worshiping with the Methodists down the road. Some said he was trying to heap burning coals on Sheriff's head with all that do-gooderism, but whatever it was, it worked. Sheriff eventually gave in, said it was Cassie's life after all.

Cassie's walking out of the bathroom now, smiling, as people look up from their plates of cake or cocktail shrimp. Some remember Cassie when she was a little girl, but she's got a little one of her own now, though her little one's not so little. Jessica's her name, and she walks step-for-step with the bridal party, making her way in stiletto heels. She's got long legs; smells like cotton candy; wears too much makeup; flirts with older men. Young thing's four inches taller than other girls her age. Boys say she's easy, and Cassie worries what might happen in a year or two when Jess and her friends get their driver's licenses and take to the road; worries, 'cause, to her way of thinking, driving's dangerous.

Cassie remembers the night Sheridan waited for her in the parking lot, revving the engine of his silver convertible, a confederate flag draped over the back seat. Dale Earnhardt's cardboard face swung from the rearview mirror as Sheridan blasted REO Speedwagon, clipped his fingernails. Cassie mopped the floor and counted cash, keeping an eye on that shiny new convertible through the painted store window. Sheridan was in a hurry to take her someplace else. And that's what cars'll do, Cassie thinks: take you places; places you might not be ready to go.

Despite the heavy makeup, the canary yellow dress, young Jess gets lots of compliments from Southern ladies in hats, but she's got an ugly scowl on her face as her mama waves like Miss America doing a victory lap, a cupped hand usually reserved for beauty queens or royalty.

When it's time for speeches, the groom, Andy, gets up. The reception is in a church hall with floor-to-ceiling windows overlooking Hartnett's empty factories. There's bunting everywhere, and lots of clean tablecloths. It's a grey September day, a chill in the air, as red-haired Andy clears his throat and says, 'we've been on a real journey together,' and, 'it's taught me to be a man,' and 'I'm taking on lots of responsibility, but I'm ready,' and 'let me end with this from 1 Corinthians,' and so forth. Andy's mama is crying again – unclear if it's out of joy or sadness – and Andy's new stepdaughter, born when Andy was just ten years old, is working her cell phone, texting a photo of herself in black thong underwear to a boy her mama's never met and Jessica hardly knows. But it's Sheridan who stays front-of-mind for most. Given his performance earlier, and the mostly negative impact he's had on the bride's life, he manages to loom over the proceedings like The Thing Which Shall Not Be Named. But when the bride takes the microphone, she manages to come closest to calling a spade a spade.

'I am just,' Cass says, pausing to fight back tears, then waving a hand, putting a palm to her mouth. She can't go on; has to give the cordless over to Andy. But as she regains her composure a minute later, she takes the mic again and finishes strong, just like her daddy taught her to. 'I'm turnin' the page. Thank ya'll for helping me do that.'

It's not much, but it's the closest Cassie gets to admitting this is her second trip to the rodeo, and that Sheridan has literally just pissed on her wedding day, practically ruining it. The assembled applaud, and someone shouts, 'amen!' Her daddy, necktie gone, says, 'atta girl.'

The reception ends with a collection of photos of Cassie and Andy projected onto a plain wall. It's so bright in the room they're hard to make out. It's all set to a song with the chorus, 'these are the best days of our lives', with most of the photos from the past year, when the couple started dating. There are baby photos of the two, as well as ones of Andy from his Christian college days, two years removed. Lots of white-teeth kids with clear skin cheering on the home-team. For Cassie, there's a gap in the photo record between birth and last year, except for one of Cassie and Jessica from six years ago: Cass kneeling, Jess in a lacey dress.

After an hour's drive, Cassie and Andy arrive in the Smokies. It's a cabin with an outdoor hot tub like the one they saw in the brochure. They walk inside and turn on the outdoor floodlights to see what's what. It's dark as a cave in the mountains; feels like you can touch every star, but even millions of those only offers so much light to see by. Cassie's never been hot tubbing, but has wanted to go for years. Fact is, she's so eager to get in, says they should take a soak before bed, buck-naked. Andy doesn't object, though his first reaction is, 'You serious, Cass?'

They open the glass doors and step on the deck, disrobe, get the jets on. Andy examines his pale legs as he slides his boxers down. He thinks of how he and Cass took vows to remain virgins till their wedding night, with Cass's vow based on a secondary-virginity she'd learned about from church-folk who'd made mistakes with sex. But it was difficult, that, given how Cassie called her daughter *a gift from God*. How do you call her a gift and a mistake at the same time? Most understood what she meant, though: easy to see giving yourself to Sheridan as a big mistake, and just as easy to see Jessica as a real treasure.

Cassie now says, 'turn the lights off', by which she means the floodlights, controlled with a switch just inside the glass doors, and Andy obliges. There are only stars to see by now, and the small artificial lights that shine underneath the hot tub bubbles. The lights make the water look like exploded fireworks as Cass moves her hand over to Andy's white thigh, but there's a rustling in the tree line, ten feet from the deck.

'What the hell was that,' Cassie whispers, pulling back.

There are two yellow eyes in the distance that glow like moon slivers. Andy can feel his heart thumping, his stomach lurch. There's a low growl coming towards them now; Andy thinks he might piss himself.

'Wolf? Bear? Oh, please don't be a bear. Please don't be a bear.'

Andy pees everywhere, but due to the chlorine, the bubbles, it goes unnoticed. Whatever it was – wolf, bear, stray dog – it retreats into the brush. When they're sure it's gone, Cassie slides beneath the water, relieved, while Andy talks like an excited teenager. Cass can't hear him, though, her ears against the jets. There's solace in the muffled rush of water. Cass dreams of growing an aqualung, leaving life on land.

The next morning they're off to Cade's Cove, a slice of natural beauty not to be missed. Only problem is they've shown up on a Saturday just as the leaves are turning. The narrow road is bumper-to-bumper with people going twenty-five miles per hour, gawking at picture-perfect meadows and old frontier churches. One sign near a weather-beaten cabin says PRIMITIVE BAPTIST CHURCH with *1821* carved into it.

Andy turns on the radio and finds a Southern Gospel station – not difficult to do around these parts – and eases the window down, resting his elbow on the car door like his dad used to on family vacations. The morning sun feels warm on his forearm, and the Gaithers are on the radio, or someone similar, singing, 'Because He Lives.' Andy used to be in a Gospel group in college, and knows the song, even hums along.

When it gets to the chorus, he tries to impress his bride with his clear tenor voice, but Cassie says, 'Hun, mind turnin' that down?' That's code for Andy to stop singing. Cass says it's 'cause she's got a headache, just like she had last night, when, after they towelled off and climbed in bed, Andy wrapped his ankle around hers, then put his hand on her hip, then moved his fingers to her inner-folds, only to have Cass turn away.

'So tired. Plus I've got a headache. Such a long day, hun.'

Andy fell on his back, saying, 'No, no, you're right, really long day.'

He looked up at the beams of the cabin till he fell asleep, thinking of a million things: the wedding, Sheridan, that animal, some deep instinct to spread his seed. Andy now turns down the radio and hears:

'Shit, hun!'

He slams on the brakes.

There are squeals of tires on pavement, the grinding of metal. Two cars ahead have just had a minor fender-bender, and there's the smell of burning rubber, a thin veil of smoke in the air.

Andy puts the car in park and steps outside with Cass. There are maybe a dozen tourists gathered around now, pointing at a red wolf as it bounds across the road, after its partner, away towards the mountains.

A heavy-set man in a checkered shirt says to anyone interested, 'I'll be darned! It's a red wolf, two of 'em! Ranger said they were extinct in the Smokies. Tried to reintroduce 'em years ago, but they didn't take. So he said at least. Them were red ones! I'm sure of it!'

The crowd buzzes with excitement.

One woman begins taking photos with a point-and-shoot, but lacking a better lens, she'll have no evidence to speak of – just something that looks like Big Foot or the Loch Ness monster.

'One looked like a female. Maybe they're breedin'?' says a bearded, broad-shouldered man standing next to a Dolly Parton look-alike.

The checkered-shirted guy laughs: 'God-willin', they are!'

People slowly get back in their cars and the line gets moving. The fender-bender is pushed off the road as far as possible.

One car's still smoking.

Back at the cabin, Cassie's got the TV on.

It's been a long day: Cade's Cove, nine holes of mini-golf built into the side of a hill, and a trip to a place where people can experience the Bible first-hand, with wax figures of Jesus going through his passion.

The Bible Experience ends at a clearing in the forest with a fifty-foot tall cross funded by a millionaire named 'Sweetie,' now passed. Sweetie made a killing in railroad transport, brochure says. There are lots of benches there, and a boulder with John 3:16 painted on it. It's all part of a bigger area with flowers and wood chips and the Water of Life Fountain. Idea behind it all is for people to stop and think about why Jesus had to die. Cass sat for ages with her head bowed, breathing deeply. Seemed she could spend the whole afternoon there, but a half-hour into it, Andy made the mistake of asking her if she'd like a sweet tea from the Scripture-themed café, five minutes' walk away – a place called *Samaritan's Lodge*. Cass snapped, 'Can't you see I'm in prayer!'

Andy shook his head and went and sat in the Lodge by himself, thumbing through a glossy brochure of mountain attractions while wondering if he was an annoying person to be with, or if Cassie just had other things weighing her down, things that had nothing to do with him, though, now that they were married, did involve him in a way.

Andy knew he had a chance to be ten times the husband Sheridan ever was, but he still had his doubts. Not about Sheridan: Sheridan scared him, no question, but that man had violated his probation so often, that, given his latest arrest for pissing in a church building and indecently exposing himself to the public, he was set to go to prison for a long time. Of bigger concern was how Cassie could've chosen someone more handsome and interesting than Andy was, and still could. He sees the way others look at her, notices how she dresses; the way her bikini underwear sometimes peeks out over her tight, low-slung blue jeans.

Fact is, Andy wasn't the only one in Hartnett chasing after her.

There was that former quarterback of Cass's high school team, looking for a wife after cancer got the first one, not to mention a young, eager leatherneck, just back from Iraq, recently separated and searching the horizon for someone to help him work out the frustrating loneliness and slaughter he'd experienced in the desert. That guy kept showing up to church, too, making long conversation with Cass after the service.

Andy can also feel heads turn when they walk into restaurants and movie theaters. In those moments, it's clear to him that he's a boy in a man's world: thin, weak, un-schooled in the way things work. It's why he spent most of his time at the cross praying Psalm 23 – 'thy rod and thy staff, they comfort me' – odd for a Honeymoon, but sensible maybe.

Cassie finally found Andy in the corner of the Lodge, looking lost, watching people chewing burgers overflowing with ketchup, drinking Cokes as big as trashcans. Andy's hands were wrapped around a tall cup covered with the word *Samari-Tea*. He was feeling badly about how things had progressed thus far in the marriage, or hadn't, but Cass put her hand on his and smiled. He smiled back, thought the clouds had parted.

Andy now walks into the bedroom with designs to make a little romance. He's just sprayed something called Pacific Wave over those parts most likely to need it after a day of walking. Pacific Wave smells like a pine forest covered in sunscreen, a pungent smell, but there's no reaction from Cass as he enters her airspace. Andy looks up at the TV, where Cass's eyes are glued, to see what's so interesting. There, the studio audience hollers with fist pumps and catcalls as a woman beats a painfully thin-looking man with a purse. Words on the screen say, 'He cheated on his wife, not only with her SISTER, but with her MOM, too!'

There are guys in black polo shirts with tree-trunk arms restraining the combatants, sending them back to their corners.

Cassie shakes her head.

'People need the Lord.'

Just then, Cassie's cell phone beeps, and she gasps as she looks at it. Andy asks what's wrong, but she can hardly speak with worry. She hits some buttons, puts the phone to her ear, but there's no answer.

Now she's running to the kitchen, rummaging through drawers and envelopes, throwing papers in the air, over her shoulder, cartoon-like, as if she's looking for a diamond in a dumpster. She manages to text with her free hand once she finds what she's looking for. Again, she puts the phone to her ear; after a few rings, there's no answer. She leaves a frantic message: 'Daddy, call me A-S-A-P about my baby!'

Cass uses language that'd make a sailor blush – *shit* this, and *mother fucker* that. Andy's heart races: he has no idea what to do. He finally grabs her hand and blurts, 'What the world's going on?'

Cass frees her hand from his grip, violently turns away, lets out a flash-flood of tears the likes of which Andy's never seen. A paper falls from her grasp to the floor: a rental contract with the cabin's address.

'Something's happened to my Jess! Sheridan says there's been a car wreck! I'm just heartsick! Must be where daddy and mama are now. Oh, God, I'm just heartsick. Oh my baby, my little baby, in a wreck…'

'Good Lord,' Andy says, 'but Cass, you sure? I mean, why wouldn't your dad call? Why Sheridan but not your dad? Your dad would call. Who was she with? Was she out with friends, or was she out with…'

But Cassie, wild with rage, turns on Andy like a wounded animal.

'He's a loser, *but he's my baby's daddy!*'

It's as if Andy has attacked her family in a moment of crisis, a family he's not a part of. Next he knows, there's a rusted convertible out front, top down, honking its horn. Cass pushes past Andy, flings open the door, runs to the car in a white t-shirt, breasts bouncing like big bowls of Jell-O. The convertible's a two-seater, and Cass yells, 'We're going to the hospital!' Andy stands there, shouting, 'What hospital?'

And then she's off: Sheridan revving the engine, peeling away. There's a moment when he switches from reverse to drive where Sheridan's eyes meet Andy's. In that moment, Andy swears Sheridan sneers at him. Makes the hairs on his neck stand up. Something cold-blooded in the man's look, way his mouth droops into a natural scowl.

Andy waits there for a good two minutes, looking at nothing in particular – his eyes are having trouble focusing on much of anything – as dust from the getaway car falls back to earth and settles bit by bit. For lack of anything better to do, he steps inside the cabin like a limp windsock; there, Cass's cell phone vibrates urgently on the bed. Andy picks it up, offers a weak hello, and hears Sheriff, mid-sentence, yelling, '...the sam-hill are you talking about! Jess's fine! She's with us!'

Andy can't even get any words out. There's bile coming up his throat. He now looks at the TV. It's the 6 o'clock news with the caption, 'RED WOLVES SPOTTED' and a live helicopter shot of two animals somewhere in the mountains, running towards a cabin. A sexed-up news anchor says the DNR wants to tag them for tracking. From the corner of the TV screen, Andy sees men with tranquiliser guns closing in on the animals as their fur pinwheels to the thwaps of helicopter blades.

The cabin's shaking now – the Sheriff's yelling, 'Cass! Cass!' – as Andy looks through the glass doors, into the eyes of a shivering wolf.

'Cass!'

A gunshot sounds.

'Cass!'

The wolf falls without a yelp.

Russell Jones

Body Rub

On Sunday I roll over
your back with my knuckles.
You're not dough and kneading,
but hazelnut butter, slowly melting
into my palms. *Higher, deeper,* you say.

I take breaths to remember the delicate recipe.
For a while we're silent and I'm baking
my finger tips in to your shoulder blades.
You've a duck egg in your spine,
brown sugars along your left side.

Eventually we must end
but as I rise up you whisper *Not yet.*
Lower, slower. And I return to work.

Apparition in a Storm

There's a speck on your tail
that might say something

about you. We're in the daisies,
next to no daffodils, waiting

for the clouds to pass
across us, between us.

Are you watching
too? We perch

by that towering statue
and the world is falling.

Watch the leaf tumble,
the breeze die. What an air

to throw. You ask for the earth
to break and it does.

I'll stay with you, then,
as the statue

is painted darker by the rain
for a darker world.

Lament for a Lost Son

my boss visits her son's grave
every night, lights a candle
in his memory
in her memory

I watch as she punches
holes, stacks papers,
parts of her
in the cemetery

the dead, like so many
rays of light
have passed
through our fingers

Salvage Crew

Won't you remember me
in the garden, the bright birds
bending the sky
toward us?

Remember the night our eyes played
on the vista, how our lips flew
in the warm evening

and if you remember the horizon
then place my silhouette
beside you.

The flowers are closing, this day's
roots are withdrawing and we
are the last of the light
on its petals.

Reviews

Mother Courage and her Children. Smokestack Books ISBN 9780957574762.
£8.95
Bertolt Brecht, translated by Tom Leonard

In Seamus Heaney's poem 'Clearances', dedicated to the memory of his mother, Heaney recalls her attitude to language and in doing so reveals his own:

> Fear of affectation made her affect
> Inadequacy whenever it came to
> Pronouncing words 'beyond her'. *Bertold Brek*
> She'd manage something hampered and askew
> Every time, as if she might betray
> The hampered and inadequate by too
> Well-adjusted a vocabulary.
> With more challenge than pride, she'd tell me, 'You
> Know all them things.' So I governed my tongue
> In front of her, a genuinely well-
> Adjusted adequate betrayal
> Of what I knew better. I'd *naw* and *aye*
> And decently relapse into the wrong
> Grammar which kept us allied and at bay.[1]

Tom Leonard will have none of this. His take on the mother tongue is very different. Reviewing *Outside the Narrative* (2009) for *The Morning Star*, Andy Croft characterised Leonard as 'William Carlos Williams meets Brecht with a Glasgow accent'.[2] Croft was not the only critic to sense that Brecht was one of the creative forces behind Leonard. In his magisterial *History of Scottish Literature*, in the section entitled 'Hard-wearing Flowers', Robert Crawford sought to connect developments in different forms of modern and contemporary writing: 'In McIlvanney's *Docherty* working-class Scots speech is kept in its place by a highly literate narrative voice whose more or less standard English dominates the text. However, in Scottish theatre working-class Scots became for several playwrights the dominant linguistic medium. Often plays presented to 1970s audiences the radical history passed over in Scottish schools. Other dramas were set in contemporary factories and workshops. On the continent the theatre of Brecht, in works like *Mother Courage*, had spurred explorations of working-class perspectives using songs as well as speaking parts'.[3]

The influence of Brecht on Scottish drama isn't hard to find. Scotland has a history of radical theatre, and of political drama inspired by Brecht, including Liz Lochhead's *Mary Queen of Scots Got Her Head Chopped Off* (1987). Yet particular playwrights, like John McGrath, occasionally chose to distance themselves when overly obvious parallels were drawn, partly for political reasons but also out of a desire to assert their own distinctiveness. As McGrath explained in an interview: 'Brecht's theories were very, very interesting, but when you're trying to create you need a certain arrogance, and I felt I knew better what was going to work for me in the theatre from watching a good performance of Brecht than from reading the theories. In terms of theory, I was much more excited by [Erwin] Piscator than by Brecht. What Piscator was saying and his accounts of productions were very exciting because they were breaking down theatre conventions'.[4] By contrast, in an interview in *The Guardian*, David Greig observed, 'you get the sense Chekhov nurtured his ideas, whereas Brecht was "Try a bit of this, try a bit of that." I'm definitely the latter type'.[5]

In 'Hard-wearing Flowers', Crawford goes on to link the ways in which 'Scottish drama of the 1970s had placed urban working-class speech centre-stage, and […] Tom Leonard's poetry had made the sound and implications of such speech resound in poems from the late 1960s onwards'.[6] The evocation of Brecht in a discussion that embraces the poetry of Tom Leonard appears prophetic now. Leonard's version of *Mother Courage* is only a few months old as I write, yet it has already had at least two public airings in the form of rehearsed readings at the Tron Theatre for TalkFest on 5 April 2014, and the following evening in the Mitchell Theatre as part of Glasgow's Book Festival, Aye, Write! The talented cast assembled for the readings by Playwrights' Studio Scotland brought Leonard's highly charged poetry to life in a beautifully vivid way. I was lucky enough to be in the audience at the Mitchell, and the combination of Brecht's powerful political drama and the integrity of purpose and clarity of expression in Leonard's poetic rendition made it a memorable evening. The event entailed a partial performance of selected scenes alongside a question and answer session with the author/ translator chaired by Graham McLaren, Associate Director at the National Theatre of Scotland. Reading the text of a play is a different experience, especially in the absence thus far of a full staging of the piece, but what is clear is that Leonard has not only captured the richness and depth of Brecht's drama, he has done more than this. I went back to the original and saw things in it that I hadn't noticed before.

Leonard has form as a translator of great European and world drama, having penned a powerful version of Chekhov's *Uncle Vanya* in 2002. Of that experience and process Leonard recalls: 'There was the basic problem that I can't read Russian, so "Brass Neck!" would be the cry from the stalls. But I set off to arrive at a performable version with something of my own sense of linguistic music set as listening device to eight previous translations. These might at the least offer me bearings on the attempts at meanings separately angled-towards by the eight separate previous translators'.[7] Anyone coming to his version of Brecht who knows Leonard's work will be less concerned with how good his German is and more interested in how his complex awareness of class, drama, history, language, music and politics have fused with that of his source material. You don't need a brass neck when you've got iron in your soul. Leonard approaches Brecht as a radical poet approaches a political soulmate.

Language is both battleground and spoil of war in *Mother Courage*, as Leonard explains in his preface to his translation of Brecht: 'The language, integral to the core of the whole, is hopelessly agenda-corrupted. In a world, and a drama, cancered by the insatiable drive for profit be it in cheese or arms, language must be likewise cancered too: the only compassionate person on the stage, the only person who is capable of instinctively loving children from the heart and of sacrificing her own life for others, is Kattrin – and she cannot speak. [...] the true hero of this play is the language in which it was written. But it is an anti-hero'.[8] Few writers can listen to the silences and subtleties of language like Leonard, as he has shown time and again – from *Intimate Voices* (1984) to *access to the silence* (2005). All poets are language poets in a sense, but for Leonard the sound of silence as well as speech is at the heart of what he does, and that makes for powerful drama. As he says of his translation, 'To have Mother Courage speak in the working class idiom of Western Scotland and urban Glasgow speech was a natural choice for a Glasgow writer like myself. The language could offer phrases and turns of speech, sardonic humour and class-rooted comment to parallel [...] the original'.[9]

Perhaps the previous work of Leonard's that comes closest to capturing his achievement with *Mother Courage* is *Reports from the Present* (1995), because what Leonard has done in this translation is to remind us that the original play is a report from the present, a report on the endless war on which capitalism and imperialism depend for their survival. As he tells us in his preface, 'It is

Brecht's play itself that with the passage of years has become template for this war that never goes away. The place and time of the play's occurrence is the place and time in which the drama, and this endless war – on stage and yet outside the theatre – presently occurs'.[10]

In the reading of Leonard's translation that I attended, it was the urgent musicality of the piece that shone through, like a protest song at an anti-war rally. Writing about war in a Scottish context without slipping into clichés or sentimentality or submerged jingoism is no easy task.[11] This new version of *Mother Courage* will last for the same reasons as the original – it speaks to us, all of us, in the here and now:

> Wi aw its dangers an stray bullets
> this war drags on from day to day
> the war could last a hundred years yet
> yet common sojer willny win.
> pure crap his food, his gear his rucksack
> the regiment docks hauf his pay
> an though it might strike you a wonder
> this war will never go away!
>
> It's springtime noo! move on your way
> the snaw's aw gone. the deid lie deid
> but you that huvny died as yet
> the powers that be, they still do need.[12]

This theatre of conflict is a war of words as well as weapons. As Leonard said on the night of the Mitchell reading, the language of the media in representing the endless war we're saddled with is 'shite'. In this context it takes both bravery and brilliance to make poetry out of it. Reviewing Leonard's *Uncle Vanya* in *The Guardian*, Lyn Gardner observed: 'Tom Leonard's juicy version is novel in […] filtering the Russian psyche through both a Scottish sensibility and a Scottish vernacular. It has its own rough poetry, with a whisky warmth rather than a vodka coolness'.[13] Gardner may be pleased to know that there's ice as well as fire in Leonard's Brecht. I hope it gets the full staging and extensive tour it deserves.

Endnotes

1   Seamus Heaney, 'Clearances', Michael Fallon and Derek Mahon (eds.), *The Penguin Book of Contemporary Irish Poetry* (Harmondsworth: Penguin, 1990), p. 169–70.

2   http://www.tomleonard.co.uk/main-publications/outside-the-narrative.html.

3   Robert Crawford, *Scotland's Books: A History of Scottish Literature: A History of Scottish Literature* (New York: Oxford University Press, 2009), p. 642.

4   'From Cheviots to Silver Darlings: John McGrath interviewed by Olga Taxidou', in Randall Stevenson and Gavin Wallace (eds) *Scottish Theatre Since the Seventies* (Edinburgh: Edinburgh University Press, 1996), pp. 150–151.

5   Maddy Costa, 'Charlie and the Chocolate Factory: David Greig on making a musical to rival Matilda', http://www.theguardian.com/stage/2013/jun/18/charlie-chocolate-factory-david-greig

6   Crawford, *Scotland's Books*, p. 669.

7   Tom Leonard, 'Translating *Uncle Vanya*: A Programme Note', *Translation and Literature*, 12, 1, Modernism and Translation (2003), pp. 155-158.

8   Tom Leonard, 'Preface', *Mother Courage and her Children*, Bertolt Brecht translated by Tom Leonard (Middlesborough: Smokestack Books, 2014), p. 7.

9   Leonard, 'Preface', *Mother Courage and her Children*, p. 8.

10 Leonard, 'Preface', *Mother Courage and her Children*, p. 8.

11 See for example David Archibald, '"We're just big bullies..." Gregory Burke's *Black Watch*', *Drouth* 26 (2008), pp. 8-13.

12 Leonard, *Mother Courage and her Children*, p. 119.

13 Lyn Gardner, 'Uncle Vanya', http://www.theguardian.com/stage/2002/may/03/theatre.artsfeatures.

X. Gallery Press, 2014. ISBN 9781852355760. £11.95.
Vona Groarke

If Vona Groarke's *Spindrift* (2009) was, as in the last lines of the title poem, 'all a kind / of love song', the task of *X* is 'to learn how a life may come to rest / on the absence of a life'. What is X? It is at once 'a shape/ signifying nothing / but a puzzle of itself' and 'Brushstroked husband / and brushstroked wife', a family 'cornered, quartered, hinged' ('X'). *X* comes to terms with the end of a relationship, trying to find language for the moment 'lover' becomes 'ex'. It is a brave and vulnerable undertaking, and Groarke charts with subtlety and poise the aftermath of a shared domestic life broken in two. Where *Spindrift* dwelt on water and transatlantic connection, Groarke's sixth collection of poems comes inland to the suburban garden and the solitary landscape of the heart. *X* also embarks on the painful endeavour of answering at least one of the questions asked in *Spindrift*: 'Am I nothing without love?' ('Power Cut'). Another 'Aubade' appears, this one in self-conscious resistance to the stanzaic shape, metre and tone of the earlier poem's depiction of the intimate gestures of lovers at dawn. The prose poem 'Aubade' of *X* reveals 'a wish to stopper up a ticking wound with consonants and vowels' and the poetic image itself 'rattles like a blown bulb' on the pillow next to the speaker alone in bed.

The title poem is arresting, aided by a free verse style that uses line and stanza breaks deftly to detail breakdown and turn certainties to doubts. Its strategies of misdirection uncover the untruth hidden in declarations. Despite the claim 'no circle in sight' in the straight lines of the letter 'x', the poem's final image is of circling and stasis: 'the blades of a bedroom ceiling fan / come to // a perfectly obvious stop'. In a volume that confronts an ending that is anything but, Groarke's capacity for a wry kind of humour peeks through in this final phrase. The epigraph notes that Descartes' *La Géométrie* associates the last letters of the alphabet with unknown quantities, and the title poem imagines the symbol first as fused lovers, then the mark of a couple at odds, a 'skewered union' undone. In '3', the speaker muses on 'My house of uneven numbers' and 'my children's hyphenated lives'. Here the serenity of a July evening is gently unravelled, 'everything supposedly given to light, / despite the slip in every corner / with a May date written on it // by ghosts who listen to everything, / but cannot make sense of it'. The dated slip shrouds the volume with a sense of foreboding, and calendrical time interrupts the seasonal rhythms elsewhere observed through the lengthening of shadows, the drooping of leaves in winter slumps and the gradual emergence of colour in the flowering garden.

'The Garden Sequence' is an extended meditation on sorrow, renewal and the passing of time, as with the 'gardens that forget themselves [...] only to turn out their box of tricks / at the first tilt of new light' ('The New Garden'). 'The Garden as Event' observes 'two kinds of hour', one narrow and sequential, the other 'stretched [...] like the skin of a drum on which / someone is keeping time, bald time, / with a persistent heart'. In this series of thirteen poems the speaker absorbs herself in the cultivation of a suburban garden, at times attaining a kind of intimacy with the flowers and shrubs tended and, at others, recognising her absolute insignificance with astonishing force: 'All this happens, is happening / without me'. The garden is a source of attention and absorption, 'a way of shuffling months / as if they were tarot cards'. The speaker prays that the garden 'absolve / each trace of my desiring' but the ghosts that crowd the poems following the sequence remap the traces of desire and memories of love momentarily forgotten. Groarke paints with the blue of cornflower and bluebell, at times turning vibrant colours pale: the white poppy and yellow bud of 'The White Garden' fading into an unanswerable existential question on the colour of loss after beauty:

> but what colour
> is the colour of where
> the last moon used to be?

In 'The Garden as an Island Approached by a Tidal Causeway', water 'unpick[s] [...] geometry'. Struts flood, structures give way, soil rises and the speaker anticipates watching, powerless, as 'all my scheme and wager / come undone'. The vulnerability displayed here is carried lightly. The speaker stands 'in my bare feet'. The colloquial turn of phrase eschews literariness ('barefoot' or 'in bare feet'). The speaker admits her need for labour and control, of 'marshal[ing]' geraniums and righting false starts, understanding the motivation for such absorption: 'life, on its own, / is not nearly enough'. By slipping 'into the ink of assembled flowers' and 'papery blossom', ('The Blue Garden') Groarke muses on confession and contrivance and, as in 'Architecture', our attraction to the perceived solidities of structure. 'The Garden in Sentiment' paints a romantic scene in which lovers exchange an Albertine rose bud for a kiss in a sentence that unfurls over eleven lines and tenderly observes the lacing and straight-pinning of the flower onto a work-suit lapel. The sixth two-line stanza prises opens a chasm of distance between the remembered scene and the speaker's present-day garden, and the declarative sentence of the twelfth and final line erases the Albertine in the absence of such intimacy. Vulnerability is itself marshalled here, though the flower's reappearance later in the sequence underlines the impossibility of erasure when it comes to memory and desire.

Groarke's self-consciousness about the confessional risk of the volume's undertaking enables her to achieve aesthetic distance from the emotional contours of the volume's thematic concerns. 'Taking an Interest in the Decorative Arts' shows her caught in an impossible either / or – 'The motif / is either artifice or else sincerity' – while, in 'Furrow', 'Pages flutter […] ornamentally' and the poetic line is 'only a matter of sound / before elision, or collapse'. A cluster of poems cast a wry look at the transparency of poetic form and symbol. In 'On the Potential Uses of Detail' accurate description of the 'composed room' is merely a method of withholding, and there is irony in 'the business of proportional reveal' in 'How to Read a Building' (which begins: 'Don't.') This capacity to reflect on the process of image-making ensures that the volume's confessional aspect is directed towards shape, colour and design, and the volume concludes in painterly mode with 'The Hammershøi Sequence'. These fine poems marry X's cool reflection on composition with intense feeling. Emotions seethe beneath the Danish painter's canvases of seascapes and landscapes, calm interiors and empty rooms. In Hammershøi's paintings and Groarke's final sequence, solitude, loss and love are subtly encoded in geometry, light and shadow. These ekphrastic poems bring to a skilfully orchestrated conclusion a volume that is as moving as it is poised.

Gail McConnell

A Lovely Way to Burn. John Murray. ISBN 9781848546516. £12.99.
Louise Welsh

One of the techniques available in a storyteller's toolbox is the retarding
device, by which an author slows down the trajectory of a narrative. Such
dilations are especially common in mystery fiction – not just plot twists but
other forms of obstruction that delay the solving of the crime – red herrings,
witnesses who die, letters and voicemails that fail to reach their destinations
– detours and dead ends on the journey to narrative closure. Welsh's major
retarding device in *ALWTB* is known colloquially as 'the sweats', scientifically
as V5N6, an H1N1-type virus spreading throughout London; one of the
challenges to readers is to determine the extent to which the sweats are
retardant, and how much they are central to the mystery at hand, in which
a shopping channel TV presenter, Stevie Flint, attempts to account for the
non-sweats death of her lover, Simon Sharkey. Their relationship, largely
physical, is detached from their respective communities, foreshadowing
society's disintegration. Also dead in advance of the virus are a distressing
number of children suffering from cerebral palsy on whom Simon and his
colleagues were testing an experimental treatment. After Simon dies, Stevie
learns he wanted her to retrieve a computer of his and place it safely in a
colleague's hands, leading her to suspect that his medical research is a factor
in what may be suicide or murder.

A quick glance at the booming genre of apocalypse stories (subgenre,
pandemic) shows a divide between those which revive the undead and those
which choose not to repopulate their deserted landscapes with zombies
(Think *The Plague* versus *The Walking Dead*, *Survivors* versus *28 Days Later*),
the latter retaining focus on practical and technological struggles rather
than threats from an easy-to-hate-and-kill population of exoticised others.
Indeed, zombies offer an easy stand-in for the global 99 per cent – poor,
huddled masses left to fend for themselves as wealth becomes concentrated
in a shrinking plutocracy, their inarticulate, mindless desire to consume
threatening any enclave of the restrained, abstemious civilised. *ALWTB* is
mercifully devoid of zombies, though the fact that the novel is billed as the
first in a planned *Plague Times Trilogy* leaves space for them to devour what is at
present a less sensationalistic investigation of the dystopia that coils, waiting,
already present, beneath orderly society. As the elliptical prologue, one of the
most evocative parts of the novel, suggests, even before the sweats, 'the city
was beginning to turn on itself'.

This personification of London offers one of the thematic pleasures of the novel, via its recurrent evocation of urban landscapes in evolution, from the ex-council high-rise 'designed with the proportions of the 1960s working classes in mind... on the economical side for the *Übermensch* who had displaced them' to the Westminster underground station, whose 'original interior had vanished beneath a monumental steel-and-concrete façade designed to remind travellers that this was a feat of engineering'. Welsh's London doesn't have the visceral geographic specificity of her evocations of Glasgow in her compelling first novel, *The Cutting Room*, but it nevertheless dexterously envisions the city as a living organism, yet another victim not only of the sweats, but also of the contemporary desire for space and privacy. Some of the most terrifying scenes in the novel are those when recent iterations of the city's layout – cul-de-sacs, for instance, or divided motorways, or flats meant for lone inhabitants – leave Stevie exposed and vulnerable. The sweats in this context become Welsh's physical manifestation of social ills, her evocations of desolate streetscapes more haunting than her characters.

To be sure, the novel isn't always all that interested in the sweats as an epidemiological phenomenon, often using it more as a plot device, to the point that much of the narrative trajectory could take place even if there were no pandemic. The infection merely exaggerates what Welsh depicts as an already-present tendency for society not to pursue answers when they don't change outcomes. As in *The Cutting Room*, the solution to the crime here doesn't promise that any killer(s) will be brought to justice or any policy changes will be made. Rather, Welsh's idealistic protagonists in both books find themselves compelled by loyalty to the dead, by a sense that stories should be complete. As in so many mysteries where killers are not apprehended by authorities, justice serves as a principle much more than a social practice. This sentiment can be read as a pessimistic view of the criminal justice system, and one of the enjoyable philosophical questions *ALWTB* raised for me was, in a world without functioning law enforcement, what difference it makes who killed whom, since the past cannot be undone.

Like readers, Stevie needs to know the answer even if there will be no consequences. Suspecting that Simon's apparent suicide is not one, she pursues her investigations through various parts of his life that he did not share with her, from family to illicit habits to old school chums to workplace politics. Obviously it is not my job to disclose which or what combination or factors are relevant and which are retarding devices, but throughout, the effect of the sweats is mainly to amplify pre-existing social conditions; what

Welsh sees in a dystopic pandemic is not so much a break with civilisation as a logical outgrowth of its flaws. Life during the sweats is nasty, brutish, and short, much like it was before the sweats.

While the novel stands as a complete narrative in itself, it also serves as the opening act of a trilogy, and as such, it is structured to be less than completely satisfying. Stevie's survival thus far makes her important to those seeking to curtail the sweats, and it will be interesting to see how far Welsh proceeds down the path of blaming Icarus-like scientists for flying too close to the sun. Such distrust of scientists dates back at least as far as Frankenstein, and its root seems similar here – men (yup, men) who seek glory, the practice of science itself an act of hubris. There's an ersatz fundamentalism to the contemporary distrust of empirical research and double-blind trials, and *ALWTB* exhibits tendencies in that direction, raising questions about why evil geniuses in search of power and money would actually enter epidemiology as a way to feed their greed: wouldn't international finance be easier, not to mention more lucrative? But like bad cops who press for convictions they know to be false, some of Welsh's scientists care less about truth or curing people than about recognition, a far less plausible plot element than the pandemic itself, with those characters some of the least convincing. Stevie's investigations of the cadre of men surrounding Simon fail to generate sustained suspense, and at points the novel drags. Narrative interest is better sustained by Stevie herself, especially when she reflects on gender and beauty.

If *ALWTB* traffics uncritically in narratives of negative progress and old stereotypes (An obligatory mad scientist? Check. Motivated by glory, fame, and fortune? Check.), such negative images of the sciences are at least partially counterbalanced by a pronounced belief in their centrality and importance, for truly, only research can save us. In the post-religious world Welsh's characters inhabit, the only deity is science, and only the truth will set you free. The need to find the solution is cast as our fundamental human enterprise, with Stevie as our stand-in. (Still, knowledge does not equal happiness: At one point, a bookie compares Stevie's hunt for answers about Simon's death to the quest for scientific discovery. "'People always think they need to know. What's betting the sweats were made in a test tube by someone who needed to know something?... Just like Eve with that bloody apple.'") Progress is cast as a myth at best and a malevolent force at worst. Overall, while not Welsh's strongest book stylistically, *ALWTB* succeeds in offering compelling reflections on the futility of human existence and a fun escapist read.

Mary McGlynn

The Architect's Dream of Winter. Dedalus Press. ISBN 9781906614782. 12 euros.
Billy Ramsell

Poets living in the Irish Republic and published in that country too don't always have the easiest time acquiring a readership beyond its borders. Poetic conversations across the different parts of these islands can be like static-infested phone calls, making any dialogue difficult to sustain. For many critics with an interest in the subject, Irish poetry still means Northern Irish poetry: the lingering cordite whiff of the Troubles is not to be sniffed at, even today. A poem by Paul Muldoon about a car parked in a gap is really all about political violence, we think, whereas a poem on the same subject by someone from Carlow or Crossmolina is just that, a poem about a car parked in a gap.

All that aside, who are these poets from the Republic of Ireland in need of a bit of a boost? Billy Ramsell, for one. *The Architect's Dream of Winter*, his second collection, is a likeable and impressive assembly. Just as Bloodaxe have done for Peter Didsbury and C.K. Williams titles down the years, Dedalus have printed Ramsell's book in larger than usual format to accommodate some very long lines and other typographical oddities. Ramsell gets us started with a list of instructions (has anyone else noticed how established the imperative tense has become as an attention-grabbing technique?): 'Surface. Cleanse yourself. Dress.' I'm reminded of Justin Quinn, of whom more anon. The first poem is called 'Secure Server', the first of innumerable technological references. Informationism was originally a Scottish invention, but Ramsell mounts a convincing bid for the Irish franchise here.

Music is a ubiquitous theme too, and in 'Jazz Weekend' we learn that 'The piano speaks the language of machines.' 'Repetitive Beats' is a description of a rave (if I'm getting that right) where the Dionysian rites of youth culture have become integrated into networks of information flow and control. It's all very *Brave New World*. In 'They dance to keep from falling', a series of marginal comments imitates those annoying requests computers send us to download new versions of this or that. We're not just reading the text, we're reading it on sufferance, and expected to play along with any requests that might be made of us. A tender interaction with some gannets is juxtaposed with the words 'Your session has expired' just as the poem breaks off. It is the technology that is really having all the fun, not us: 'Light flushes and reflushes its brittle cocoon. It desires. / The circuits whisper and it dreams our name.'

By the time we get to 'Memory House' and its self-distancing, opening line ('I outsourced all my memories to machines'), we might wonder whether

The Architect's Dream of Winter is the Irish slim volume retooled as a sequel to *Blade Runner*. Must the unhappy replicant always dream of being human? It would seem so, to judge from 'A Net of Limes' ('But soon, my friend, soon, I'll emerge from this circuitry') and 'Colony' ('The machines have entered the language, my love, entered us'). Still, releasing the genie from the bottle takes some doing. I'd begun to worry Ramsell was heading for an endless hall of mirrors of hyper-reality when the fine elegy 'Henrietta Street' surprised me with its human-all-too-human qualities. As suggested, this is a formally diverse assembly, with 'Ahead vast systems hunger' a practically Prynneite open-form sonata. Ramsell works in educational publishing, and in 'Section 3: The Unseen Poem (100 Marks)' he manages to pull off the old trick of the meta-poem (in this case a poem in the form of a Leaving Cert unseen text plus questions) without managing to seem naff. I hereby just about forgive Ramsell for his use of the 'You do this, I do that' format in 'Glitch', as recently seen in Simon Armitage and Nick Laird poems, and the blame for which I am pinning squarely on 'Love Song' from *Crow*. It may be time for this format's Captain Oates moment, minus the vague promise of return.

One problem with the discussion of standard versus non-standard lyric forms in Irish poetry is the trotting out of the same few names on the non-traditional side. Justin Quinn's *Fuselage*, for instance, his left-field third collection (much of it, coincidentally, on the same technological themes that so engross Ramsell), appears to have bypassed critics whose radical touchstones remain the 1930s generation of Coffey, Devlin and MacGreevy. It seems very much an influence here. Ramsell's affection for medium-length-to-longer poems on musical and hedonistic themes may owe something to Alan Gillis, of this parish, and has the effect of pushing his work into unusual, lyric-stretching shapes.

The Architect's Dream of Winter is very much a mischief-making collection. It has vigorous humour, independent spirit and narrative brio – an impressive combination, by any standards. Non-Irish readers curious about what's going on in the Republic, press 'refresh' now.

David Wheatley

Moss Witch and Other Stories. Comma Press. ISBN 9781905583423. £9.99.
Sara Maitland

In May 1949, C.S. Lewis sent the finished manuscript of *The Lion, the Witch and the Wardrobe* to his goddaughter Lucy Barfield. In the package he included a letter which became the book's dedication when it was published the following year: 'I wrote this story for you,' he said, 'but when I began it I had not realised that girls grow quicker than books. As a result you are already too old for fairy tales, and by the time it is printed and bound you will be older still. But someday you will be old enough to start reading fairy tales again.' If there is a writer today who proves that fairy tales are not just for children, it's Sara Maitland.

Moss Witch and Other Stories gathers together fourteen stories inspired by conversations with scientists about their work. Each story is followed by an afterword written by the scientist. In this structure, it mirrors the anthology *When it Changed* (Comma Press, 2009), in which the title story 'Moss Witch' in fact first appeared. *When it Changed* is a variable collection, in which the tales frequently fail to create a compelling story out of the science. There, 'Moss Witch' stands out not just for its quality, but for its genre. Whilst the other stories are science fiction (with the exception of Patricia Duncker's mystery 'The Bellini Madonna'), Maitland's story is a fairy tale, a literary genre that falls into the broader category of fantasy.

For most mainstream readers, science fiction and fantasy are one, conjoined as they are on bookshops' genre shelves. But within the genre world, it's a very different story. Perhaps the most famous theorist of science fiction, Darko Suvin, is vehement in his distinction between the two – both, he says, estrange us from the world in which we live, but science fiction does so by logical extrapolation from scientific fact, whereas fantasy by definition eschews scientific explanation. Many people disagree with Suvin, but it's a distinction that's proved hard to leave behind. Which is what makes Maitland's collection so interesting. For she has managed to bring together science and literature, and produce not science fiction, but compelling fantasy. She is, it could be said, the Heston Blumenthal of the new trend for sci-art collaboration: she brings together oxymoronic flavours – snails with porridge, bacon and eggs with ice cream, caviar with white chocolate, science with folk, fairy tale, parable and myth – and produces dishes that unexpectedly please the palate even whilst the incongruity of their combinations is not disguised.

Take, for example, 'The Beautiful Equation', an intriguing story about twin brothers who return to living together again as adults after their mother dies. Derek and David are identical, except for the fact that Derek has Asperger's Syndrome. He becomes obsessed with a scientific equation which means nothing to David, nor in fact most readers. This is where the scientific afterwords come in handy, since they explain in more detail the scieantific background to the stories – the equation, Dr Tara Shears explains, is Dirac's, and led to the prediction of antimatter, a hallmark of which is that 'when it touches its matter equivalent, both annihilate'. When David returns from holiday to find all the walls covered in the equation, he loses his temper and launches himself at Derek: "'MYSTERIOUS DISAPPEARANCE OF IDENTICAL TWINS" said the local paper the following week'. David and Derek, as the latter has intuitively understood, are exactly the same, its just he 'spins the other way' – they are matter and antimatter, and their physical contact brings about its necessary conclusion.

'The Beautiful Equation' is a story of queer intimacy, of the relationship between brothers who are somehow both identical and opposite. This theme permeates many of the other stories in the collection. All are created out of an experiment with the intimacy of science and literature, but this interest in unusual combinations, in exploring the possibilities – and perils – of queer intimacies, becomes a repeated theme across the stories, not just the method of their creation. In 'Seeing Double' a boy grows up protected, for as long as he can be, from the knowledge that there is another face on the back of his head, a vindictive female face that upon her discovery eventually harries him to his suicide; in 'Her Bonxie Boy' a female scientist specialising in migratory sea birds falls in love with one of them who, in an expansion of the Scots selkie myth, is a skua at sea, a human male on land; in 'Moss Witch' the conflation or transgression is not between human and fauna but between human and flora, as a bryologist's passion for moss leads to his gentle murder at the hands of the Moss Witch. (In the story 'Far North' from her 2008 collection of that title, it's clear that Maitland's fascination with the particular horror of tender taking out is endebted to Tennyson's brilliantly disturbing dramatic monologue 'Porphyria's Lover').

Other stories bring a lighter, comic note to the collection: 'How the Humans Learned to Speak' is a wonderful origin story which attributes the development of language to the human need to bond via laughter due to larger group sizes making grooming, the traditional method of bonding, impractical; 'Jacob's Sheep' takes the biblical story of Jacob and Rachel winning a flock of sheep from her father Laban and explains their triumph via Rachel's curiously advanced knowledge of genetic engineering. What these two stories also have in common with each other, and with many others in the collection, is that the scientific innovator is a woman. Maitland is a proud feminist – she was part of the feminist collective that produced the feminist short story collections *Tales I Tell My Mother* and *More Tales I Tell My Mother* in the 1970s and 80s. Whilst the Moss Witch, and the collection that shares her name, speak 'the language of science and turn... it into a love song', Maitland stands high on the hill of twenty-first century Western literature and culture, opens her mouth wide, and exhales a powerful and fertile feminism which it is hoped will, like the Moss Witch's spores, be 'caught by the wind, and carried up into the higher air currents that circulate the Earth. And then...well nobody knows'. Such is the way in which Aunt Ann explains the effect of feminism on world culture – slowly, surely, perhaps often unseen – in 'A Geological History of Feminism', although this story uses an extended metaphor drawn from plate tectonics theory. In this sense Maitland's collection is in keeping with the spirit of the times, in which the Royal Society is sponsoring Wikipedia Edit-a-thons to write the role of women back into the history of science: 'Lighting the Standard Candles' tells the story of Henrietta Leavitt, whose discoveries were fundamental in helping astronomers measure the scale of the Universe, but who was treated merely as one of the Observatory Director's 'girls' rather than a 'real astronomer'; 'Anaka's Factors' is as close as any tale in the collection comes to science fiction, in which a lesbian couple use stem cell biotechnology to persuade one of the women's stem cells to become a spermatozoon and thus to conceive a child together. 'Instant Light' and 'The Mathematics of Magic Carpets' – both beautiful stories about the intimacy possible between science and play, thought and love – extend this project of rewriting the history of science by including within them the tales of scientists who are too often left out of the Western grand narrative.

Only one story in the collection falls flat: 'On Sneezing an Uncertain Sneeze', whilst also starring a funny female scientist who is also not just a mother but a grandmother, ultimately fails to spin a story from the science. The remaining two stories, 'The Metamorphosis of Mnemeosyne' and 'Dark Humour' are both interestingly self-reflexive, since both are concerned with the role of story telling in our personal and collective lives. As final stories so often do, the latter gathers together many of the key themes of the collection: science, literature, intimacy, women's liberation, and, in amongst all that, the possibility of children. Einstein famously said, 'if you want your children to be intelligent, read them fairy tales. If you want them to be more intelligent, read them more fairy tales'. To adapt Einstein for the twenty-first century: boys and girls, young and old, if you want to be intelligent *and* enlightened, read Sara Maitland's feminist tales.

Sarah Dillon

In Secret: Versions of Yannis Ritsos. Enitharmon Press. ISBN 9781907587214. £9.99.
David Harsent

David Harsent's take on Yannis Ritsos is from the Robert Lowell end of imitation rather than translation. Just as Lowell's Rimbaud, Baudelaire *et al* sound distinctly Lowellian, the Ritsos of *In Secret* is presented with a voice readers of Harsent's previous collections will tune into immediately. That's not to say that imbibing all of this Ritsos hasn't had an impact on Harsent's diction – these poems are noticeably leaner than his most recent collections: gone, largely, is the slant-rhyme and long musical line, replaced by a terser, more tight-lipped cadence. These are poems free of poeticising, or heightened register –instead they're spoken in a spare, conversational tone, closely tied to the possibilities of the speaking voice and its intimacies of address. The English poet this Ritsos has most in common with is the Harsent of *Dreams of the Dead* or *News From the Front*, but despite this reining-in of some of the ballad-inspired strides taken since the early 1990s, it doesn't feel like Harsent running in reverse. Without those collections which have come since Harsent lengthened his line in *A Bird's Idea of Flight*, the lessons of control, constriction and revelatory gesture he's learned in an expanded prosodic landscape, he could not present a voice whose sorrowful restraint sings out so fully, and for which 'sleek and naked/ absence' is a most beguiling muse.

Some of the keynotes of any Harsent collection are the ominous sense of threat lurking just out of sight, of psychological trauma barely resisting declaration, of things being always on the brink of collapse. In Ritsos, the politicised and perennially interned Greek subversive, Harsent has found an ideal alter-ego to mine something new from these obsessions, and a number of poems which, like Harsent himself, refuse to go in for pomposity, generality or emotional excess. In 'Blocked', 'Words are defined by what they dare not say' and it is this phrase which serves as something like a creed for the Ritsos we encounter here. Understanding that the act of writing, and of bearing witness, is itself protest enough, the Ritsos whom Harsent presents to us is unwilling to sacrifice art on the altar of sloganeering subversion. The power of these poems – a power, accumulative and in isolation, which is at times staggering – comes from their restraint, from what is left out, and from the irrefutable notion that 'You could tell/everything from the way they dipped their heads'. Harsent's mastery of implication and his ability to create an atmosphere using the simplest materials is given a shocking charge by the world he gets to inhabit through Ritsos. The interior scenes of rooms, mirrors and windows not only look back to Harsent's *Marriage* and its charged domesticity but to the earlier era of *The Review*, and its championing of Imagist-inspired interpersonal poems which 'legislated for tenderness' in Hugo Williams' phrase. While Harsent never entirely went in for those single, shining moments, his talent for crafting a necklace of short poems which set up a narrative built on observable, concrete symbols, was the perfect apprenticeship for presenting Ritsos' Greece where 'sheets smell of goodnight' and 'She turns away with the striking of the match, /walking towards the kitchen, her face in shadow, her back /bent under the weight of so many dead –'.

As well as claustrophobia, scrutiny and a sense of what might count as paranoia if we didn't know the truth of the matter, there is also an air of imminence, and reckoning, which emerges throughout. The first hint of this, which is a further nod towards Ritsos' *ars poetica*, comes in 'The Trial', where 'When they think no one's looking they let the fragments fall. / The dead man's mother, wrapped in her black, collects the crumbs – / evidence for when the survivors come to trial.' The poems, like these crumbs, may not appear on the surface like much of a protest, but through their cumulative observation and refusal of the obvious, hysterical motion, they not only serve to conjure and condemn the mood and atmosphere of Ritsos' oppressive era, but to transcend documentary reportage. Through this insightful looking at the seemingly ordinary it becomes clear that a much darker truth can be discerned, such as in 'Double' where the fact that 'There are two of him, one inside the other' is discovered because 'you'll see him lift the fork /to his mouth slowly, /steadily, as a mother does /when feeding her child.'

Aside from the odd bit of dateable detritus – 'cola cans' etc – these poems almost operate outside of time in its most prosaic, limiting sense. This idea is hinted at in 'The Crane Dance' where 'things change: new passions, new threats, new fears' but 'people still dance that dance: just common folk, / those criss-cross steps that no-one had to teach.' What Harsent has managed to extract from Ritsos is that same stripped back, human 'dance' – by focusing on the small detail and the human action within rooms, close to home, Harsent is able to tell us about how oppression, fear and injustice affect us all; by this personalising method these poems become universal, as in one of the 'XX Tristychs' where 'The entire city reflected/in your emerald ring'.

The hints set up in 'The Trial' never, like anything else in this collection, turn into explicit proclamations, but the air of homecoming, of there being some hope that this state of affairs will pass, is strengthened in a number of places, not least by the presence of that symbol of restitution 'Penelope', where 'The grave-cloth she'd worked to destroy /hung on the frame like something flayed.' In a more pervasive sense, though, it is the lingering, ghostly presence of the dead, again adding to the sense of these poems' ability to be above, rather than limited by, time which points towards an unlikely but enduring hope against this darkest of backdrops. 'Helen' opens with the statement that 'The air in the house is made heavy by the presence of the dead', and indeed the dead linger, sitting down for meals or begging the question in 'Philoctetes' 'Who can tell /what is ours and what belongs to the dead?'

The dead aren't only ancient presences, of course, but the many killed in Ritsos' time, for whom these crumbs were gathered in order that they might get some posthumous justice. The modesty of Ritsos' work finds its aptest analogy in one of the most bracingly affecting lines of the collection – 'Our heroes are small men, pasty-faced and fat.' Harsent, by virtue of his extraordinary talent for razor-sharp observation, allows Ritsos' steely, unflinching look at horrifying injustice to not only retain its power and dignity, but to bear witness all over again to both specific and global truths about persecution, and to a poet who, like the characters in 'The Dead House', was willing to 'sit here until the fires burn out.' This is a collection of exemplary poems which never resort to cheap tricks or vulgar gimmickry to beg for attention. They have no need – the quiet, surgical voices of both Ritsos and Harsent ensure we are rapt throughout, thanks in large part to their never rising above the level of ordinary speech.

Declan Ryan

The Rental Heart and other fairytales. Salt Publishing. ISBN 9781907773754. £9.00.
Kirsty Logan

Who needs fairytales? In the reality TV age surely we are all our own best
objects of fantasy, all substitutes in the big bingo game of life, cheering on our
avatars to ever more ludicrous undertakings. Who needs morality tales in the
free-market of the self? There was a time when fairytales expected to teach
us something – about life and conduct and moral and sartorial correctness.
Charles Perrault in the first written fairytales would end his stories with a
lesson learned, that the tale of Bluebeard, for example, schools girls not to be
curious. Who needs fairytales indeed!

Such grand efforts to control meaning are, we like to think, a thing of the
past. However, revisiting the fairytale acquiesces to its power and attempts
to retrieve its treacherous undertows for new and contemporary revelations.
Ask Angela Carter, who Kirsty Logan cites as an influence. To be fair to
Kirsty, it is only on the cover that the stories in this collection are referred to
as 'fairytales'; inside they are simply 'other stories'. This equivocation justifies
pointing out that they are, in fact, somewhere inbetween, a story land of no
particular parameters.

The twenty stories are a mixed bag of writerly influences. Some directly
re-write traditional narratives: 'All the Better to Eat You With', 'Matryoshka'
which re-perceives the Cinderella story, and 'Sleeping Beauty', for instance,
which tells in reverse the effects of an act of sexual abuse between a woman
asleep and a casual acquaintance. In this short scenario, the protagonist of
the title has as much agency as the fairytale character and, in addition, is
reliant on public opinion: 'She'd be That Girl. Did you hear? She was asking
for it.' In other cases, fairytale characteristics crop up to orientate the reader
– Baba Yaga – only to lead them to unexpected resolutions. Other stories are
fantasies of the weird and macabre involving mechanical love objects ('Coin-
Operated Boys'), the circus, the eating of words or lightbulbs. Some stories
would like to be fairytales but can't help emphasising their entrapment in the
gauntlet of very material female oppressions. 'Momma Grows a Diamond'
sets a girl's coming of age in her mother's brothel while 'Underskirts' tells the
story of a Sapphic Lady finally committed to isolation in a religious institution
by her husband; 'the contemplation of darkness will help her better than the
touch of a hand ever could' on the pebbled road to heaven. Perrault could
not have put it better. Yet other stories play out a founding concern with
desire and loss without recourse to outright fantasy, only the stripped down

essentials reduced to a reverberating image ('The Gracekeeper') or a wayward desire ('The Broken West').

The overall effect is kaleidoscopic, where shifting colour and tone are foregrounded over stability of time and place. This is important for the ultimate aim of this writing: to open wide the possibilities of interpretation. These stories often have intangible meanings and inconclusive endings which confound our understanding. Like words with the vowels omitted, they are suggestive and evocative, testing and teasing. Gap toothed as they are, they still fulfil our narrative desire; while blanking our wishes they encourage intellectual quests. And the crucial thing here is escaping the heteronormative shackles of the real world. Many kinds of desire are in play – for all combinations of gender, kin, love objects animate and inanimate – highlighting the kinks of the nearly-normal, meaning all of us. In their attention to emotional detail the stories often demonstrate how fragile our sexual norms are; just changing a putatively small detail – the gender of a paramour or a quest-seeker – can subvert the foundations of our most embedded social system. The moving story 'A Skulk of Saints' recounts the birth of a baby boy to a female couple, an event that brings them in from the social margins. A need for warmth and light and home marks this relationship, normalises these individuals in a deeply demarcated world. How normal is the extraordinary in these cameos.

And for the most part these are consoling narratives which don't quite leave the comfort zone of love, couples, and a yearning for the normal. Though they can be dank enough, with trees 'vomiting leaves', the most recurring image here is the red valentine heart. This yearning could make being inconclusive into being non-committal; sometimes too many gaps leave you toothless. The exciting questions arise, of course, not in relation to the presence of the normal in the extraordinary, but with faith in the extraordinary itself. Logan is aware of this; in her metafictional moments she hints at our power to escape the normal, not least in the final story, 'The Tiger Palace', which ends, 'But, as it turned out, stories can have any ending you like.' This opportunity is her gift to the reader; she is offering in this collection a radical spirit on the point of revealing itself.

Carole Jones

Pelmanism Luath Press. ISBN 9781910021231. HBK £12.99.
Dilys Rose

Near the close of Dilys Rose's stingingly well-observed new novel, Gala Price and her Gran sit down to an evening of card games on a felt-top table. They begin and, as it turns out, end with Pelmanism. The rules have each player facing a full pack of cards spread face down across the table, each selecting two at a time, the aim being to collect all the pairs; the player with the most pairs wins. The 'skill is in memorising where certain cards lie, and improving on chance'. Thus, the game, and the complex scene to which it belongs, captures some of the central issues of a novel which precisely explores the price of memory (its pleasures, pain and denials) through a family (Price) of the same name.

Of course the book's title also evokes the self-help system of memory strengthening advertised widely to Britons in the first half of the twentieth-century, many of whom, like Gala's family, were at the same time irrevocably traumatised by memories of their experiences in two world wars. Famously, the mail order instruction manual they received was in most cases too lengthy, perplexing and dry to inspire any further engagement. Rose's novel, on the other hand, offers a precise, moving and humorous attempt to capture the erratic workings of memory within the intriguing inter-chronologies of its plot. It is crafted through an array of scenes and characters which call forth the language, spaces, sensations and habits of mind of a past which is still recent enough to present itself sharply through familiar smells, tastes, emotions, tunes and turns of phrase. Yet its distance and potential to constitute a burden is marked by the growing 'silt of memory' which the narrative always knows it is up against..

The novel is centrally focalised through Gala, a daughter whose return to Scotland during the Thatcher era to visit her now mentally failing father, bookends the novel around a series of short, vivid chapters which dart about in time. Her twin touchstones as she grows are her father and her Gran, each of whom is dramatised in the opening chapters of the novel where death and water forge an unforgettable series of associations in Gala's head. In the first Gala has a memory of her quixotic and tyrannical father Miles staging a spectacular dive through a ring of fire at an open air swimming pool, after which he 'posed, Olympian, by the diving tower' and the 'ring of fire flickered like the halo of a dark planet'. Yet in recalling the event Gala is 'not sure she really saw the show', only that 'it was mentioned often' by her father. Her own mental image memory of the event punctures her father's myth-making with a deflationary account of his 'drippy, droopy trunks... eyebrows slightly singed' and accompanied by a smell of 'kerosene and scorched rope'. By contrast, the next chapter features Gala, this time the foolhardy protagonist, following her father's example (but not his words of warning) as she ventures, still unable to swim, into the deep end of the same pool by walking along the submerged boundary wall that separates it from the sea. She succeeds, only to fall over in the shallow end where she is rescued by her Gran who manages to evacuate the 'brine and bile' for her mouth and stomach and promptly administers 'hot orange squash' from her flask before she 'magicked a dark disk wrapped in waxed paper. A treacle toffee'. Gran is the 'dear, familiar voice' not only of this scene, but of the novel and indeed a wider culture for whom these two forms of sustenance conjure up ineffable pleasures; outdated, even undesirable in the present but part of system of past family comforts whose unique smells and textures are the very fabric of childhood memory. By contrast, Miles leads his family through a perpetual crisis of financial and social embarrassment as he embarks on endless and hopeless opportunistic artistic reinventions and schemes (variously as a sculpture, potter, water colourist, oil painter). In doing so he provides the narrative with a series of dramatic and often spectacular scenes in which denial, alcohol and self-delusion form the foundation for a pattern of destructive forgetting. Meanwhile, Gran's presence, habits and acute attention to the present moment (the key skills of Pelmanism) constitute an unseen rudder: 'Without Gran steering the family through its own deep waters, the house tipped and rolled'.

The central achievement of this novel is the beauty and precision of its attention to how the past feels (its colours, smells, mobilisation) and how we feel our way through these to it. It includes wonderful idiomatic phrases and disappearing verbs which light up the prose. A dog, for example, is 'a wild-eyed squitter of nervous energy', Gala is described as 'plittering about in the shallow end' of a pool, her Gran is never without a 'poke of sweeties', and her friend Lil sends her apologies to her fellow cards players when 'she cracked her dentures on a lamb chop and couldn't thole the mortification of being seen on the bus with a caved-in face'. In the process *Pelmanism* brings to life small, disappearing and deeply unfashionable lives; it makes space for door-to-door salesmen hawking 'crocheted tea cosies and antimacassars' around suburban bungalows, incorporating both trauma and tenderness as it goes.

Helen Stoddart

What Long Miles. Bloodaxe. ISBN 9781852249656. £8.
Kona Macphee

What Long Miles by Kona Macphee is a delightfully esoteric collection of poems. The reader is beckoned on with questions and jovial asides, yet an element of the poems is bodily, and distinctly eerie, reminding us of the unsettling, unexpected and often fatal. A sense of an overarching theme in 'What Long Miles' is perhaps elusive however the smaller thematic groupings of poems within the anthology are both fascinating and effective.

One of the earliest poems in the collection is 'Prodigal', a longer text of five eight-line stanzas which implicates the reader directly in its musings, the anaphoric 'Would you…' illuminating Macphee's vivid description of a life errant, of 'some heady freedom, going your way / on a whim or a coin-toss'. 'Prodigal' is particularly skilled in the way it bridges many of Macphee's thematic preoccupations within the collection – the 'open road' of landscape; the 'crazed engine' of scientific interest and the question of what comes at the end of a journey: 'the empty, dirty palms / of the hands upturned in a mocking question, / the feet that bore you nowhere, here?'.

From 'The Great Wave' through to 'The new order' the shift turns to environments and catastrophe – 'The Great Wave' itself sings 'of structures / smitten to their fractured elements' while the post-apocalyptic landscape of 'The new order' looks at the repercussions of such cataclysmic events. Again, Macphee's attention turns to journeying, to the synecdochal feet 'pressganged […] then seeped / as blisters ruptured on that stricken march'. The journeys Macphee describes here are ones of uncertainty, of unease and horror. The notion of emotional baggage as well as physical toil is intertwined within this narrative, as Macphee comments that 'we couldn't ditch our heavy stash, of family snaps / nor hazard them a look'. This wry comment indicates the irony of memento in such situations – we carry them, Macphee notes, despite their inaccessibility and impracticality.

'Dry County' and 'Inland' are a particularly effective coupling. 'Dry Country' depicts an agrarian, desert landscape, and the emotions such an environment evokes – 'the smell of *far*' and 'the pull of *yearn*'. The 'sudden wet' which appears all too briefly and dissipates all too quickly in the space of the final two lines speaks to the desire to grab something nourishing and transient. 'Inland' pulls the natural imagery of rivers and inlets into an urban context, allying the city to a body of water where 'at nightfall, every full-moon streetlight / dons its yellow glare; there are no tides'. Macphee shows an unnerving knack for amalgamating the technical and the natural in her lyrical and vividly descriptive poetic style.

Macphee's use of language startles with its ability to evoke an almost visceral, empathic reaction from the reader. This is particularly potent in the poems written for a 'Scotland & Medicine' commission. The 'sliver by revolting sliver' of 'Meat' provokes a singular disgust in the reader, while the ghoulish content of 'George Pirie's hands' depicts a slow-burning horror, reminiscent of 1950s images of nuclear fallout and gasmask fears. Though the poems are unsettling, there is no doubting Macphee's astonishing capacity for the uncanny amalgamation of the scientific and the corporal.

Two poems seem to bridge this particular skill with her ability to capture human character – 'Soldier and piano' and 'Scheele's Green'. While 'Soldier and piano' echoes back to 'The Great Wave' in its dystopian vision of an environment harrowed by conflict, the keen juxtaposition of pure art (the beauty of the piano) amidst the literal wreckage of a brutal war is stunning,

> […] casting up this music
> like a shell-pocked wall: forgetting the blank staves
> of the future; forgetting, at his back,
> the crooked double bar-line of his gun.

Macphee has chosen to add some explanatory notes at the end of the text, and in the case of 'Scheele's Green' this is an interesting and effective decision. The additional information about Napoleon's exile and the eponymous poison dye that played a part in his death illuminates further the lamentations within the text, of empires lost, with the elemental decay of the human body played out in his memories of defeat and conquest.

In many senses the strongest poems are the shorter poems which showcase Macphee's loquacious and dry wit. 'Office Suite' is a triptych of short poems dealing with office mundanity: 'The commute' speaks to the paralysis of the Monday morning return to work, where 'the chanted sentence of the rolling stock / offers no remission, no abridgement'. 'The labour' would not be out of place in the aesthetic of Terry Gilliam's 'Brazil' – 'the sub-committees burgeon, spawning hydra heads / with toothless mouths, a thousand aimless screeds of paper' and the concluding section 'The compensation' reduces the weekend to a poignant set of images, encapsulating the routine of the nightclub, the high street and the sofa.

This artful brevity is mirrored in 'How to fail', a delightful poem which again illuminates Macphee's proclivity for gentle, yet dark, humour. There is something defiant and beautiful in her instructions to 'tattoo the purple / of a hammered thumb' and 'vaunt / the bum note ostinato' and the concluding stanza rings with a glorious humanity:

> Get back on that wagon,
> That wild-eyed horse.
> Fall into the sunset.
> Dust your britches. Hum.

These shorter poems convey a great talent for short, sharp images yet other poems such as 'Prodigal' indicate that Macphee's talent is more than adequately matched to works of a more prosaic style.

Changing the thematic focus, 'Against melancholy' is a harrowing image of the devastation of depression, 'the deadening, the silencing elided as you name / your dark as *melancholy*'. The 'muted waymarks' of Macphee's verse within this poem evoke a distinct mental torment. 'Singularity' speaks of the slow encroaching darkness of depression, 'its growing wrap of absences, / the faces, places, anecdotes that mutely disappear'. 'Minifesto' combines the sparse verse of the more comic poems with the vivid imagery of the darker subject matter. It is a strictly divided poem which depicts the 'void-mouthed beast' of a mind divided. This poem is structurally brilliant with the conflicting images physically set apart on the page, inviting the reader to read the poem time and time again as disparate parts, each their own narrative, and as a mutually informative whole, not unlike a fractured consciousness.

In all, 'What Long Miles' is an evocative collection by a skilled poet, whose wit and prowess as a wordsmith are reinforced by the artistic and nuanced poetic performance within the text. The synthesis of the smaller thematic preoccupations is engaging and effective, and Macphee's poetic skill is more than capable of carrying such a varied and rich collection.

Lucy R. Hinnie

Something Chronic. Word Power Books. ISBN 9780956628367. £13.50.
Bob Cant

Bob Cant's debut novel, *Something Chronic,* follows the fortunes of Euan
Saddler who, immediately after casting his referendum vote in 1979, falls
victim to a sleeping disorder (à la Rip Van Winkle), to wake up at the dawn
of a new millennium, twenty years later. It's 1999, but not as you knew it. In
this semi-mythical late-nineties Dundee, escapee elephants roam the streets; a
radical nationalist party, 'Scotland First', preaches bigotry from the local radio
and plasters cautionary posters warning of the 'rape of Scottish culture' on
the city walls; and Dundonian teens are being sucked into an organisation
called the 'William Wallace Youth League'. Cant's Dundee is somewhere
between the early days of Nazi Germany and Brigadoon.

Something Chronic (Scots slang for something done to excess) is an extremely
apt title, neatly summing up the novel's presentation of nationalism, which
is so over-the-top as to be farcical. Yet whilst Cant's manner is not deadly
serious, the novel suggests that nationalism is a chronic condition, one that
may prove seriously deadly to both societies and individuals. The novel's
genre itself is something chronic –motioning towards magical realism, social
commentary and farce, without really committing to any of them. The
style too seems excessive: an engagingly droll, over-the-shoulder narrative,
interspersed with a voyeuristic epistolary style. (Perhaps this is no surprise
from Cant, whose wonderful compilation of shared testimony, *Footsteps
and Witnesses,* demonstrates the power of direct, first-person experience.)
But although Euan's recovery diary is a perfectly enjoyable read, it's hard to
appreciate exactly what the novel gains from this dual narrative, since the
third-person account is also privy to Euan's thoughts.

Cant's wide-eyed protagonist wakes up in a whole host of ways: politically,
and sexually too. A no-nonsense sort, his observations on societal change are
a hoot. 'Women are allowed to talk about sex too, as if it was something they
might enjoy,' Euan notes, wonder-struck. 'I don't think we had assertiveness
when we were growing up, but it really is the thing now,' he enthuses winningly.

Very much the everyman, Euan soon seems to fancy every man he sees,
and has catching up to do. This book isn't 'about' sex, but it does flash its sexy
bits with the gallus determination of a coatless lassie on Dundee High Street
in January. Euan's narration in particular might make Cant's first novel a strong
contender for the *Literary Review*'s Bad Sex award: 'he had me squatting like a

dog and pumping away inside me', but Euan's descriptions are so liberatingly free from guile, regret or shame, that – in this respect at least – it sounds like unusually good sex.

The novel's blurb declares it 'challenging', and it does challenge, in different ways, from page to page. At times it's a vernacular pop-quiz: What does a Dundonian mean by 'pan-loafy?' (toffee-nosed, if you weren't sure); and expressions like 'kent whit' add local flavour without jarring. There is a sexual vocabulary here, too, which might broaden one's horizons in ways less geographical. 'Frottaging', for instance, is one worth looking up for yourself, if you're not already *au fait*. Better still, *Urban Dictionary* offers 'frottagonist', surely a term set for mass popularity in one's dafter circles.

The novel also provides more genuinely challenging challenges. What are we to make of the mystery graffitist who, throughout the book, daubs 'Dundee is not Rwanda', 'not Srebrenica', and so on, across the town walls? The recurring motif does remind us of the bloody atrocities that nationalist and tribal fervour can give rise to, and the slogans are even printed in a different, graffito-ish font to flag up their importance, yet not one character says a thing about the genocide-heavy graffiti campaign, and I'm left unsure of what to say, either. Set in a real place, a real time, it is sometimes brain-meltingly difficult to know what is intended as satire, what is fiction, and what is a nostalgic look at Dundee. The kind of Scottish nationalism depicted in *Something Chronic* is hard to recognise, either in our political present or in the Scotland of the late nineties. The extremists within the novel are anti-immigration, massively racist and deeply misogynistic. If the novel is holding up a mirror to society, it's hard to know where exactly it is pointing. A local station, Radio Dighty, uses shortbread-tin parochialism to sugarcoat hate, and cutesy phrases like 'bide-a-wee' are twisted, in relation to asylum seekers, to mean 'get out'. As an attack on nationalism across the world, across history, it stands, and at times Scotland First even bring to mind the more memorable UKIP gaffes, but thankfully they have no obvious precedent in Scottish nationalism, and it would seem damaging and reductive to suggest otherwise.

Yet, if such extremism is hard to see reflected in party politics, the attitudes to homosexuality within the novel, whilst frequently expressed with some hilarity, ('homosexuality is as un-Scottish as vegetarian haggis') do not seem so far-fetched. As a young man in the seventies, Euan has no name, even, with which to understand his homosexual feelings, and so waking up in the late nineties, he finds his first brave trip to the town's one gay bar relatively liberating. Things have improved, but not quickly enough, and the widespread homophobia that surrounds Euan still, is the one aspect of nineties Scotland which need not be distorted to appear shocking. Seen from a queer perspective, nationalism and independence are suddenly a more daunting prospect, and it becomes clear that the fictionalised, or transposed, racial or gender-based bigotry which stands out as so glaringly unrealistic within the near-millennial Dundee of the novel are a means of helping the reader to understand what it is that LGBT communities have had to face, and continue to face.

Setting aside the objection that Scottish nationalism, as Tom Nairn notes in *The Break-up of Britain*, has long been 'unique in the world' for its 'apolitical and acultural' nature, and that if it were to develop into one of those other, darker, forms of nationalism, surely we might have seen more to indicate as much by now, *Something Chronic* conflates a desire for Scottish independence with nationalism, something which might, in our political present, be hard for many to swallow. Lakshmi, a character who serves both as generic strong female and the educated voice of racial diversity within the novel, opines that 'fantasising about independence and nationalist nonsense is a waste of good brain power'. Eat your cereal, basically. Surely Lakshmi, as the educated independent woman she is (and she is, sadly, little else), would know that brain power is like love: the more you use it, the more you have left. The independence movement, like the Scottish people, leans left in the main and has been demonstrably forward-thinking on LGBT issues, but as Cant argues in Word Power's fascinatingly diverse book of writing on Scottish Independence, *Unstated*, 'not all players accept the change of rules', and for a community still struggling towards equality in Scotland (where nearly 70 per cent of LGBT teens report homophobic bullying, and nearly 80 per cent of schools have no policy in place to tackle it), Cant's concern as to whether Scottish queer communities can trust an independent Scotland to continue to promote their complete equality seems not without reason.

As you might expect from the cover – radioactive green, with a rainbow elephant – this book has a mild psychedelic effect. That's not to say that it's a book about drugs, aside from Euan's prescription medication – which may or may not be the reason he calls a woman a turnip and believes himself to be in communication with ghosts, most notably that of John Knox – drugs feature peripherally, and are of the sink-estate 'Oh God, the horror' type, rather than the Yellow Submarine sort. No, the psychotropic quality of the novel lies more its ability to make you question reality within the book's world, and so without it. *'Something Chronic'* is surely a statement about nationalism, but sometimes it seems a vague, elusive, or fairly tenuous one. The novel frustrates and entertains in equal turns.

Katie Craig

The Temporary Gentleman. Faber & Faber. ISBN 9780571276950. HBK £17.99.
Sebastian Barry

Sebastian Barry's latest novel draws on themes already touched on in his two most successful tomes so far. As in 2008's *The Secret Scripture*, the narrator in *The Temporary Gentleman* sits down to write his memoirs; and just like in *A Long, Long Way* (2005), the First World War is a partial setting for the book.

The Temporary Gentleman might not have ended up a contender for this year's Booker Prize like those predecessors, but it's still an accomplished work. Written in the Irish writer's typically claustrophobic style, it's a short but heavy-feeling novel. Light on dialogue, large on description and occasionally slipping into stream of consciousness, it's an uncompromising piece of literary fiction – but ultimately, it's also accessible and touching.

Irishman Jack McNulty is living out his days in Ghana, shortly after its independence from Britain in 1957. It's not immediately clear why he's there or what's become of the love of his life, Mai Kirwan – who we later discover he married. But the mysteries of McNulty's life gradually unfold over the subsequent pages as he forces himself to remember and put pen to paper on the sad turns that his life and marriage have taken.

The novel is imbued with a lovely sense of poetry, the sentences gliding into one another with a comforting smoothness. Barry's novels often take a little work to settle into, but once you're there they carry you along and The Temporary Gentleman is no different.

Amidst the close-knit prose, there are some astute stand-out lines. For instance, upon encountering a friendly stranger on a ship bound for Accra, McNulty muses, 'Happy to hear an Irish accent I asked him where he was from and he said, with that special enthusiasm Irish people reserve for each other when they accidentally meet abroad, Donegal.' Later, an Irish policeman in Accra tells him, 'I tell you, half the time I'm out here, it's like I never left Ireland. Take away the heat and the fucking palm trees and the black skins and it's all just Ballymena in the rain, I tell you.'

In fact, a nostalgia for Ireland runs through the whole novel – even though the parts of the story set in Ireland are far from happy memories. McNulty and Mai's story is one of poverty, alcoholism and debt, amidst a tumultuous relationship that spans before and after both world wars. It's not an exaggeration to say that the tale told by *The Temporary Gentleman* is truly miserable. Yet it's also conveyed with love and warmth.

As McNulty continues to write his autobiography, he gradually becomes more and more aware of his culpability in his sad family history. There's one particularly affecting scene in which Mai's friend Queenie meets with him in private to discuss Mai's descent into depression and her confessed thoughts of infanticide – of which McNulty has no awareness whatsoever. His absolute refusal to believe that his wife is not just depressed but also an alcoholic leaves Queenie in tears, as she tells him in sad, tortuous detail of Mai's (failed) attempt to perform a home abortion by drinking gin in a hot bath.

These morose flashbacks juxtapose with McNulty's seemingly quiet life in Accra, with his manservant Tom Quaye. Tom also contributes to McNulty's nostalgia, as he has 'excellent English from an Irish priest who taught him years ago. Indeed, he has a bit of a Roscommon accent, which makes me homesick.'

That quietude ends when Tom takes McNulty to a local party. After a few drinks, the Irishman is involved in a fight that he can't remember. Subsequently, he receives several visits from policemen to enquire about the matter and warn him of possible reprisals. Through their questioning, we become aware that before his current stint in Ghana, McNulty had been involved in gunrunning in Togoland (which today is part of Togo and Ghana). Disappointingly, this part of his history is never explored in detail. If it were, it might inject a little more action into the last third of the book, which flags compared to its strong middle section.

These shortcomings, together with the book's dour tone and its dense imagery, temporarily makes the approach of the end welcome. But Barry turns the story on its head with a surprising twist on the last page – so surprising that it makes you want to go back and read the novel again to look for details you might have missed. Perhaps placing this plot detail at the start – or even the middle – of the novel would inject it with the quicker pace it often lacks.

Despite this thrilling finale, the relentlessly miserable tone of the book, as tragedy piles upon tragedy, might be a bit much for some readers. But while *The Temporary Gentleman* might not be one of Barry's best books, it's a tender story that's lovingly told – and could be immeasurably more interesting if you read its final page first.

Yasmin Sulaiman

Notes on Contributors

Paul Batchelor lectures in English Literature and Creative Writing at Durham University. His first book, *The Sinking Road*, was published by Bloodaxe in 2008. A chapbook, *The Love Darg*, recently appeared from Clutag. www.paulbatchelor.co.uk.

Rachael Boast was born in 1975. *Sidereal* (Picador 2011) won the Forward Prize and the Seamus Heaney Centre for Poetry Prize for Best First Collection. *Pilgrim's Flower* (Picador 2013) was shortlisted for the Griffin Prize.

Colette Bryce's fourth collection, *The Whole & Rain-domed Universe* (Picador), has been shortlisted for the Forward Prize. She is a part-time Research Associate on the Bloodaxe Archive Project at Newcastle University, for which a filmed version of this interview was made.

Cameron Conant was born in Michigan and graduated from Edinburgh University's writing programme in 2012. He lived for years in Tennessee and has worked in publishing and journalism. He now lives in Scotland and is writing his first novel.

Katie Craig is the new Teaching Fellow of Creative Writing at Edinburgh University. She writes short stories, funny poems, songs and has a new novel up her sleeve in need of publication, if you're interested.

Sarah Dillon is Lecturer in Literature and Film in the Faculty of English, University of Cambridge. She is author of *The Palimpsest* (2007), and editor of *David Mitchell: Critical Essays* (2011) and *Maggie Gee: Critical Essays* (2015).

Sasha Dugdale is a poet, translator and editor of *Modern Poetry in Translation*. Her third collection, *Red House,* was published by Carcanet in 2011.

Tracey Emerson is a graduate of the University of Edinburgh's Creative Writing PhD programme. Her short stories have been published in anthologies and magazines, and she has just completed her first novel. She works as a freelance editor and literary consultant.

Jenni Fagan is an award winning poet and novelist and poet, her novel *The Panopticon* is published in eight languages and is currently being adapted by Sixteen Films. Fagan is a Granta Best of Young British Novelist, *The Sunlight Pilgrim*s is due out next year.

Lucy R. Hinnie is a part-time PhD student at the University of Edinburgh. Her research focuses on the querelle des femmes and women's voices in late-medieval Scottish verse. She has previously reviewed for *Tower Poetry* and *Hortulus*.

Nicholas Hogg was nominated for the IMPAC Literary Award for his début novel, *Show Me the Sky*. Winner of the New Writing Ventures award for fiction, and various short story prizes, his third novel, *TOKYO*, will be published in 2015. www.nicholashogg.com @nicholas_hogg

Carole Jones is lecturer in English at the University of Edinburgh. Her interests span gender, sexuality and queering representations in Scottish fiction and beyond. She is author of *Disappearing Men: Gender Disorientation in Scottish Fiction 1979–1999* (Rodopi, 2009).

Russell Jones is an Edinburgh-based writer. He has published two pamphlets of poetry, with a series of sonnets and a full collection to follow. He is also the editor of *Where Rockets Burn Through: Science Fiction Poems from the UK*.

Jackie Kay's recent works – all published by Picador – include the short stories *Reality, Reality* (2013), the poetry collection *Fiere* (2011), which was shortlisted for the Costa prize and the Saltire Scottish Book of the Year award, and the memoir *Red Dust Road* (2010), which won the Scottish Mortgage Investment Trust Book Award. She is Professor of Creative Writing at Newcastle University.

Gail McConnell is a lecturer in the School of English at Queen's University Belfast. She is the author of *Northern Irish Poetry and Theology* (Palgrave, 2014), has contributed to *The Oxford Handbook of Modern Irish Poetry* and published in *The Irish Review*.

Mary McGlynn is Associate Professor of English at Baruch College, City University of New York. She has published on James Kelman, Roddy Doyle and other contemporary Scottish and Irish writers, as well as on film, country music, cultural studies, and Irish America.

Martin MacInnes has had three articles on natural history and identity published in *Edinburgh Review*. In 2014 he published short stories in *New Writing Scotland* and in *Gutter*, *Litro*, and *Dactyl* magazines, and won a New Writers Award from Scottish Book Trust.

Marianne MacRae lives in Edinburgh and is about to begin a PhD in Creative Writing. She has been shortlisted for the Bridport Prize four times and once saw Margaret Atwood buying an ice cream.

Willy Maley has published previously in *Edinburgh Review* on Janice Galloway, Alasdair Gray, James Kelman, Peter Mullan, and Muriel Spark. He is the author of *From the Calton to Catalonia*, a play co-written with his brother John, newly reprinted by Calton Books.

Alice Myers explores possibilities within and around documentary photography. For the project 'The Sky is Down on the Ground' she worked with a community in Mayo, Ireland, who have been combating the installation of a raw gas pipeline for twelve years. Over the course of many conversations Alice became aware of a connection to the landscape and sense of duration beyond the timescale of oil companies and photographers. www.alicemyers.net.

Nicola Nathan grew up in South Wales and now lives in the Chilterns. Her poems have been published in *Poetry London* and *The Next Review*. She is working towards *Thumbelina*, her first poetry collection.

Victoria E. Price is a lecturer in Theatre Studies at the University of Glasgow. Her publications include articles on contemporary Scottish theatre, Shakespearean adaptations, and early modern theatre and drama. She is on the board of A Moment's Peace theatre company.

Vidyan Ravinthiran teaches at Durham University. Besides academic publications – he is working on a book about Elizabeth Bishop – he reviews widely, and co-edits *Prac Crit*, an online magazine of poetry and poetics. *Grun-tu-molani* (Bloodaxe, 2014) is shortlisted for the Forward Prize for Best First Collection.

Declan Ryan co-edits the *Days of Roses* anthology series and is poetry editor at Ambit. A pamphlet of his poems is forthcoming in the Faber New Poets series.

Helen Stoddart is senior lecturer in English Literature at the University of Glasgow. She is currently working on a book about the relationship between the British post-war novel and urban space.

Yasmin Sulaiman is Books Editor and Acting Editor at *The List*.

Matthew Sweeney's most recent publication is *The Gomera Notebook* (Shoestring, 2014). His last full collection, *Horse Music* (Bloodaxe 2013), won the inaugural Piggott Poetry Prize. Bloodaxe will publish a new collection, *Inquisition Lane*, in 2015.

David Wheatley's critical study *Contemporary British Poetry* is published by Palgrave. He lives in rural Aberdeenshire.

Ryan van Winkle is a poet, live artist, and podcaster living in Edinburgh. His poems have appeared in the *American Poetry Review*, *AGNI*, and *Prairie Schooner*. His second collection is due to be published by Penned in the Margins in spring 2015.

http://www.edinburgh-review.com

Please join us on Facebook and Twitter.